The Rose Tattoo

An Intimate Memoir
on the Mystery of Love

Books by David Gregor:

In Different Times (Memoir)

Variations on All the Perfect Things (Poetry)

Hundred Waters (Memoir)

Into the Fold (Book Collecting Reference)

The Rose Tattoo (Memoir)

The Rose Tattoo

An Intimate Memoir on the Mystery of Love

by

David Gregor

GRB Publishers, Langley, Washington

2019

The Rose Tattoo

David Gregor

Published by:

GRB Publishing
P.O. Box 1491
Langley, WA 98260
info@gregorrarebooks.com

Book and cover design by Denis Zimmermann at zimmermannstudio.com

First Trade Edition
1234567890

This memoir is for Bethany Moore
and especially Rose Rydeen

Acknowledgements

I want to thank Victoria Hawker and Brent Siewert for their undaunted editorial assistance with this project; their numerous readings of the manuscript made me a better writer. Marian Myszkowski, Robyn Meehan and Alicia Elliot kindly read an early draft of the book and I appreciate the valuable commentary they provided. I am eternally grateful for Denis Zimmermann's book and cover design. Once again a tip of my hat to Susan Jensen for her keen eye for detail. My thanks to Dez Rock for allowing me the table space at Useless Bay Coffee where this book was written and edited. Much appreciation to James Michalopoulos in New Orleans for allowing me to use his painting "We Groovin'".

The Rose Tattoo

An Intimate Memoir
on the Mystery of Love

"We tell ourselves stories in order to live..."
- Joan Didion

"When you find a white feather in your path
it is a clear message your angel or a loved one
is nearby and offering guidance."
- Cherub

"Do not hide your crazy from me,
mine seeks company."
- Matthew Spenser

Chapter One
In the End

"You made me happy"
- Rose

Everything in my life has been a story: The good, the bad, and the unexplainable. No event or personal encounter ever had a simple explanation. There was always a connection to some previous incident or relationship that lead to my current situation. Life for me has not been a series of isolated occurrences but a long line of interconnected links to a larger story. As a result, it has taken me a lifetime to learn something about love and fate and the choices I've made regarding those powerful forces. As a young man, I spent little time trying to understand why certain events happened or why some people came into my life. It was all I could do to manage the present, let alone question the past. But with age, that would change, as would my awareness of a mirror soul.

Love can enter our life when we least expect it, change us dramatically, then disappear when we believe it will last forever. Life, with its matters of the heart, is full of questions but it's the answers that are not always easy or plentiful.

The awakening for me came with an unexpected encounter with the woman I was still in love with, despite our year of separation. Our love affair had ended abruptly without a satisfying explanation until that September night in 2016 when an unforeseen meeting challenged my understanding of love.

That September evening the music from inside Bayview Hall boomed across the parking lot as I approached the front entrance. To my surprise, I saw Rose leaning against the wood railing smiling at me as I started up the ramp to the front door. She was standing next to her best friend Marian and talking loudly over the music inside the hall. Rose's long brown hair was pulled up on top of her head, wrapped in one of her signature blue bandanas. Her smile was warm and inviting when our eyes met. Her slender body still defied her age, and she carried herself with the confidence I knew all too well, if not a little more tentative than I remembered. She had a hint of fragility that made me wonder if time had finally caught up with her usual exuberant presence. It had been almost a year to the day since Rose ended our love affair and now she surprisingly reappeared in my life. It was no coincidence I was at the Bayview Hall dance that September night. I needed the comfort of music and the company of friends. However when I saw Rose I sensed something important might unfold, but I didn't know whether it would enlighten or sadden me. For a year, it wasn't what was finished that haunted me, but what had been left undone. Rose, I would quickly learn, needed to see me one last time.

When I approached Rose with a tentative greeting, she deliberately embraced me and told me a friend of hers named Joanie, whom I had met the year before in New Orleans, was in the hospital. Then without any further conversation, Rose clutched my arm and led me off the porch, out into the hall's dark parking lot.

For ten glorious months we had shared a romance that brought us both what had been missing in our lives. We were in love, and we were happy. Then without warning or a satisfying explanation, Rose suddenly ended our love affair. It was no accident we had not seen each other for a year; it had just been too painful for either of us to see the other and not be together.

As we walked out into the dark lot, with the muted sound of the band playing in the hall, I was unsure where we were going and why. Rose had gone out of her way to avoid any contact with me after we separated and now she had me by the arm with something clearly in mind. I lit a cigarette and she asked me for one. The way my lighter lit her face reminded me what first attracted me to her. She had a classic, almost timeless beauty that defied her sixty-five years. Her eyes were soft, her full lips inviting, and her skin still showed none of the usual signs of someone her age. She looked twenty years younger than I knew she was, and I could feel there was a purpose to her wanting to see me.

"You look like you've lost weight," she said, as we walked.

"You look as beautiful as the last time I saw you," I said.

We approached a lone wooden bench near a large patch of pampas grass and sat down.

"It's hard to be back here," she said.

"It's hard for me too."

"Too much history," she said.

"I'm surprised to see you," I said

"I thought you might be here," she said.

"I'm usually not here," I said.

"It's been easier for me to stay away too," she said. "It would have been too painful."

"I know," I said. "You know me and places. There are too many that remind me of us."

"Not going out has been easier," she said.

"And tonight?" I said.

"I thought you might be here," she said. "I needed to see you again."

"You *needed* to see me?" I said.

"Yes."

"About Joanie?"

"Not just Joanie," she said.

I looked over at her, silhouetted against the hall's dim porch light, and felt my stomach tighten into a knot. There was so much I still needed to know about what had happened with us.

"I told you not long after we met I loved you madly," I said. "I meant it then, and I still love you."

Rose stared straight ahead without speaking.

"Tell me," I said. "I need to know. Why did you step away?"

She continued to stare off into the dark. I could feel she wanted to tell me something, but she was struggling to let it out. I resisted saying anything, wanting the silence to force her to give me the answer, the answer to why she broke my heart. I wanted her to tell me why so I could put our mysterious ending behind me and move forward with my life. She looked over at me, leaned forward and rested her elbows on her knees looking off into the chilly September night.

"I need to know," I said. "I need to know why. You owe me that much."

She continued to look out into the darkness, and I waited for an answer. I could see by the pained look on her face that whatever was on her mind, whatever compelled her to seek me out that night, was important. I continued to look at her, waiting, until she finally broke the silence between us.

"Because…," she started to say, then cut her reply short.

I waited for her to continue, but the words didn't come. "Because is not good enough," I said. "I need to know why?"

She butted her cigarette and looked at me.

"Because," she said. "Because…you made me happy."

"I made you happy?" I said. "You didn't want me in your life because I made you happy?"

"Yes," she said. "Because you made me so very happy."

That night was the last time we ever spoke to one another, but it was not our final chapter. Once again, Rose gave me a perplexing response to an honest and heartfelt question which left me more confused than ever. Her words haunted my days and nights for months, forcing me to revisit my life and our year together. I came to believe the answers to my questions lay in the events and the conversations we had shared. I needed to understand how happiness justified the breaking of two hearts. It was up to me to uncover what our late-life romance meant, and the true meaning of the word love.

Chapter Two

"Lovers don't finally meet somewhere.
They're in each other all along."
- Rumi

I have never believed in coincidences. I do however believe events in life happen for a reason. Looking back over the last seven decades, my journey has been dotted with obstacles, open doors, opportunities taken and choices made; each one in their own way provided new meaning to my life. Time after time small jogs were made with no specific destination in mind; the only things known for certain were where I had been and where I was at that moment. There was no reason to look back; every day, the moment at hand held the possibility of new encounters that could change my life—sometimes in small ways, other times with significant consequences.

In retrospect, I realized I had no predetermined plans for my life; no specific goals to achieve or grand ambitions to fulfill. In many ways I was like a cork on the ocean: I was pulled here, bounced there, periodically redirected by strong winds. But at no time did I ever see the events in my life occurring without purpose; those moments, not all of my own choosing, were part of the ongoing narrative of my life. Situations arose, possibilities were considered, choices were provided, and decisions were made.

People came in and out of my life. Some had more influence than others. My first wife provided stability after my discharge from the army. My college newspaper editor guided me through my first published feature story that garnered a national writing award. A casual comment by a former employer planted the seed that led to starting my book business in 1987. My domestic partner of seventeen years worked tirelessly on my four published books and helped me open my book business. The guitarist in my blues band gave me permission to sing and to this day shepherds my growth as a performer. Each of these influential people proved one important thing: There was a recognizable purpose to their presence in my life.

Life is a series of ebbs and flows, and by the summer of 2014, dissolution had overtaken my life. After more than a year of separation, I ended a ten-year marriage to my second wife. The toxic nature of that marriage had taken its toll on me. I had not been in charge of my life or my future, and I had clearly lost my bearings. I needed to find my life again, a life I had lost somewhere along the way. More importantly, I needed to know if a deep and honest love was still possible.

Some people come into our lives for a lifetime, others for only a season. If we are lucky, the most influential enter our life and nothing is ever the same; we are forever changed by their presence. They may bring us peace or guidance, uncontrollable laughter or the deepest affection; but whatever their gifts, they impart them for a reason, as if guided to us with an intent. They see something in us, a trait or inclination that we are unaware of at the moment. And the strongest attraction is often an important quality missing in our life. Even if their season is brief, they can change us dramatically because of the intense brevity of the relationship.

We don't always know what we are looking for in life until the day we finally find it and our life is never the same. That is the way it was in the fall of 2015, after more than a year of solitude, when another woman radically changed my life. It was my sixty-eighth year and I believed I had met or seen every type of person there is… until I met the gypsy soul named Rose Rydeen.

Every summer, a local non-profit organization on the south end of Whidbey Island sponsored a series of outdoor dances at Bayview Corner, five minutes outside of Langley. The dances drew a couple hundred locals out on a Wednesday evening to dance to live music and socialize under blue skies. I made an effort to attend all the dances that summer, if for no other reason than to see friends and hear good music. The final street dance of 2015 fell on September 10th, and I had a rare Wednesday night off from my second job.

That evening was sunny and warm, and the band was in rare form. People young and old danced into the night with a sense of the changing season and the passing of summer joy. At 8:30, the band finished their last song for the night, and I watched as people slowly headed to their cars. The band broke down their gear, and friends said their goodnights. The evening was ending with a golden glow of the setting sun, and the warm night air was too perfect to go home. I bought another beer and chatted with lingering friends.

The woman who organized the dances was a tall redhead with an outgoing personality named Marian Myszkowski. I knew Marian casually as the person in charge of booking the bands for the summer dances. I was standing alone next to the beer stand when Marian approached me with a friend and gave me a friendly hug.

"Hey you," Marian said.

"Nice event tonight," I said.

"Yeah. Great turn out. Do you know my friend Rose?"

I looked over at Rose and smiled. "I don't think so," I said.

Rose was a little shorter than me wearing a pair of skinny black jeans, a colorful vest and a fiery red sweater. Her thick brown hair was wrapped up inside a blue bandana. She wore a pair of wide-rimmed sunglasses and had the warmest smile and brightest teeth when she looked at me.

"You guys talk," Marian said. "I've got things to pick up."

I introduced myself and for just a moment felt I knew Rose, though I had no immediate memory of having ever met her. She appeared relaxed yet somewhat tentative being left with a stranger. I leaned back against the metal railing and looked at her. Nothing moved around us except a wisp of her hair caught by a passing breeze. Rose removed her sunglasses then darted her eyes away from mine. The sudden expression on her face was that of someone remembering a pleasant memory, a memory that touched something deep inside her. I looked down at her slender legs, up to her small waist and quickly at her prominent breasts under her colorful vest. A sculptor could not have carved a more perfect figure.

"So…Rose, what do you do on the island?" I asked.

Without a moment's pause, she said, "I raise chickens and grow pot."

"Chickens?"

"About 120."

"You weren't kidding."

"And you have the bookshop in town," she said.

"I do."

"And the band Deja Blooze."

"Right again. Have you heard us?"

"You did the blues opera."

"You were there?"

"Actually we met there," she said. "After the show."

"We did?" I said. "I hate to say it, but I don't remember meeting you. I'm sure I would have remembered."

"You were talking to a lot of people that night. Marian and I had a discussion about you during the intermission."

"Whether to stay for the second act or not?"

"Whether I would do you."

"Do me? And…?"

"I told her I would."

"You should have said something to me."

"You were with your wife, I believe."

"Not any more. I could have used hearing that."

She reached for my beer and helped herself to a sip. Rose's honesty and bold behavior was refreshing. I had no particular interest in chickens and had not indulged in the herb for some time, but something in Rose's attitude and her awareness of me made me want to know more. Her candor was inviting, and her voice had a soft-spoken confidence that could drive away bad spirits. The longer I looked at her the more she was like a dream I didn't want to wake up from. I could hardly look at her for long out of fear she might be a mirage, and if I looked at her too long she might disappear.

"Do you want to get a drink next door?" I said.

She looked down the walkway toward the Taproom. She swiveled around as if looking for someone, then turned back at me. "I can't," she said.

"Another date?"

"I...ah...I need to help Marian collect the empty beer bottles."

"You're going to pick up empty beer bottles?"

"Nice meeting you again," she said. "I really have to help Marian." Then, as quickly as Rose had entered my life, she turned and walked away into the night.

Chapter Three

"You thought everything is ended,
but it's yet to begin."
- Anonymous

All the way home after the street dance and into the following day, I couldn't stop thinking about the intriguing woman named Rose. I was perplexed by a woman who admitted a willingness to "do me" but chose to pick up beer bottles rather than have a drink. It was a strange conundrum. We had talked with ease and her soft-spoken directness made the conversation effortless and playful. The plainspoken way she openly shot from the hip made me want to know more. She clearly knew more about me than I did about her, and that also intrigued me.

For the last 28 years I had made my living buying and selling collectible and out-of-print books, and the eleven years I had operated my book shop in Langley had been good years. But the day after the street dance I couldn't focus on books or selling them. I kept replaying my brief encounter with Rose over and over trying to remember if I had missed a cue or if her preference for collecting empty beer bottles over having a friendly drink was her way of saying "I'm not interested."

That evening had ended in a rather unsatisfying way. Something felt unresolved, and I was bothered by not having a satisfactory resolution to what felt like a promising introduction.

The following day, I did my best to catalogue some new arrivals and photograph them, all the time thinking about that curious woman at the street dance. Even though we had only talked for a short while, I was immediately attracted to her. Part of her allure was she knew who I was which meant she had spent some time focused on me, but chose to keep her distance. She was willing to engage, but resisted taking the engagement to another level, and that decision perplexed me.

I took a mid-afternoon break from book cataloging and walked across the street to the Star Store deli for a snack. I got a cup of coffee and a croissant and was walking toward the cashier when Marian stepped around the corner in front of me.

"Hey," she said, "how are you?"

"Fine," I said. "Good fun Wednesday night."

"It was good" she said. "And the weather couldn't have been nicer"

"Looking for dinner?" I asked.

"I just can't decide what sounds good," she said. "And you?"

"Just getting a pick-me-up," I said. "Say…I enjoyed meeting your friend the other night."

"Oh…Rose is great."

"She seemed a little quiet but interesting with the chickens and the pot growing."

"I've been trying to get her out more often."

"A problem with crowds?"

"No," she said. "Her husband died awhile ago."

"Sorry to hear that. Does she live around here?"

"On Welcome Road off of Wilkerson. She has a little food stand on the road with the best eggs."

"Well, it was a fun night," I said, "and I enjoyed meeting Rose."

We hugged goodbye and I went back to the shop. I spent the next hour thinking about what Marian had told me about Rose's situation and where she lived. The few things Rose had shared with me made me wonder what had not been shared. If Marian had to work to get Rose out of the house and I didn't follow up our brief meeting, I might never see her again. The more I thought about Rose, the more compelled I felt to do something.

I grabbed a bottle of red wine I kept in the shop for emergencies and put the "Closed" sign on the shop door.

Chapter Four

"I BRUISE ON THE INSIDE."

Being impetuous had never been one of my personality traits. If anything, I had become more reserved over the past ten years, trending toward indifference especially when it came to engaging with women after my separation. The last thing I needed was another destructive personality in my life. I was just not inclined to chase after women or driven to impress anyone. The only exception to that trait was making music. When I wrote and played music I was a different person. Another side of me came out; there was no fear, anxiety or shying away from a more public persona. That was when I felt the most alive and most like the person I wanted to be.

I loved to write, whether it was prose, poetry, book reviews, or music. The process of putting observations, feelings or experiences on paper was something that gave me great pleasure. Creating order out of chaos was rewarding; I enjoyed the challenge of making something tangible out of a blank piece of paper. But for some time the impetus to write had dried up. Then to have an attractive woman prefer collecting empty beer bottles over having a drink with me just didn't sit well. Even though she had rebuffed my invitation, I felt an unnerving desire to see Rose again in case my gut feeling was correct.

The roadside market Marian mentioned was easy to find. I saw the Welcome Road sign and I pulled off the road and stopped short of continuing further. The road went deeper into the property, but I wasn't sure how far and hesitated whether it would be appropriate to just show up uninvited. I sat there at the tree line and debated whether to commit myself and continue down the road.

The market building off to my right looked new. The wood structure was professionally built with a small deck in the front with potted plants and flowers on either side of the open door. The plants were clearly tended to regularly, because there was water runoff from the containers and the flowers were still blooming. A wood picnic table with a colorful pot of flowers on it sat off to the side on the freshly mowed grass. Tall pine trees behind the market created a solid wall of seclusion between the road and the property beyond. The only break in the trees was the narrow dirt road.

The longer I sat there the faster my heart raced, and I debated whether I should continue down the road or turn around and leave. Finally I eased the car into drive and slowly drove forward into the dark heavy fir limbs that blocked out the sky over the road. The tall trees quickly thinned out and the sun shined down on a clearing accented by an even larger fir tree with a dirt driveway that circled around it. Beyond the driveway the land was cleared with a large penned off area with three small wood structures in it. To the left of the driveway was what appeared to be a barn or a large shop decorated on the outside with a big rusty saw blade, an old metal sign for Norm's Resort, and an Ice Delivery sign. To the right was a renovated double-wide trailer with wood-slat siding and a small wooden deck facing the driveway. The deck was ringed with clematis and honeysuckle vines and red and yellow rose bushes in their final days of bloom.

I stopped the car opposite the deck and was immediately greeted by a large dog that ran up to the car door barking. I grabbed the bottle of wine, slowly got out of the car and cautiously petted the dog that turned out to be as friendly as it was big. I heard a voice call out, "Bella" from inside the house. I followed the voice around to the side of the trailer and saw the side door was open. Four rough-hewn logs served as steps up to the porch landing and as I approached the stairs the screen door opened and Rose appeared above me wearing a black and white striped apron. There were small white powder splotches on her left cheek.

"Hey there," Rose said.

"I hope I'm not interrupting anything."

"Just baking some muffins," she said, wiping strands of hair from her face. "What's up?"

"Well…since you were too busy the other night collecting empty beer bottles to have a drink with me, I thought I'd bring the drink to you. And try again."

Bella jumped up on me and pushed me back a step.

"Down Bella," Rose said. "Well…you should probably come in then."

The inside of the trailer was island rustic. The linoleum kitchen floor was worn bare in places and some of the floor boards creaked. The interior window frames were untrimmed as were the door jambs. The half wall separating the small living room from the rear of the house was filled mostly with a wide screen TV. There were a dozen stuffed game birds on top of the half wall; several rifles and a shotgun were mounted on the wall of the narrow hallway leading to the rear of the trailer. Three antique pistols were displayed on the wall next to the TV.

The kitchen was compact and smelled of fresh-baked cake. A tray of muffins cooled on the six-burner gas stove that looked new and extremely professional. A dozen cast-iron pots and pans hung off a wrought iron rack hanging from the ceiling. There was a blue plastic bucket filled with eggs sitting on the counter next to the double sink. A brown-haired cat Rose called Mr. Kitty quickly darted past me and out the back door.

"Smells good in here," I said.

"We should sit outside," Rose said. She removed her apron and handed me a corkscrew from a drawer. She took two wine glasses from the cupboard, filled them with several ice cubes, and we went out through a sliding door onto a rear deck flooded with sunlight. She pulled two metal chairs around the black metal table and put cushions in each chair. The sun was warm and bright and the air was quiet except for the high-pitched whir of the hummingbirds darting in and out of the three feeders suspended from the eaves. I opened the wine, and Rose took the bottle from me.

"So, you're here," she said, filling each of our glasses.

"I was crushed you wouldn't have a drink with me."

"You don't look any worse for being rebuffed."

"Is that what I was?

"I believe so."

"Well I bruise on the inside."

"So… what did you expect by coming here today?"

"Wow," I said. "You get right to the point."

"Shouldn't we get to the point?"

"I don't know. I just got here. I'm sort of playing this by ear. I'm not usually this impulsive."

"So I brought the impulse out in you?"

"I was intrigued by the hundred chickens and the pot reference."

"Pretty exciting stuff?" she said.

"It got my attention," I said, "but then I'm easily amused."

"Easy. That's an interesting character trait," she said. "Care to smoke?"

The afternoon sun was warm on my face and off in the distance I could hear the muffled clucking of chickens. Bella had found a sunny spot next to my foot and occasionally raised her head and cocked it from side to side. Rose told me Bella was an Australian sheep dog bred for taking care of livestock and extremely protective.

For someone who just had a near perfect stranger drop in on her, Rose was more than accommodating and very much at ease. Once again I had the feeling she was someone very familiar to me. I couldn't immediately make the connection, but it gave me pause as I tried to figure out what felt so familiar. She handed me the brass pipe, lit it and we smoked and sipped our wine. She dropped another ice cube in each of our glasses, and I felt myself staring off in the direction of the chicken sounds. The warmth of the sun felt good on my face, and I felt completely relaxed.

"Are you still here?" she asked.

"I'm sorry. I just had a feeling…like I knew you from somewhere."

"It's entirely possible," she said.

"Didn't mean to drift off," I said. "You were saying…."

She told me about her market business and how between the fresh eggs, her baked goods, and her deceased husband's social security she had a comfortable life. The property was paid for and she lived modestly. It was not an extravagant life, she said, but it was a life without a lot of complications.

"I hope my coming here isn't a complication," I said.

"We'll see."

She asked about my shop and I briefly explained I bought and sold out-of-print collectible books. I also told her I was on the board of the Chamber of

Commerce, and how I moved to the island because of a woman.

"And that woman now?"

"I filed for divorce two weeks ago."

"And now you're here?"

"You make it seem wrong," I said. "For the record, we've been separated for over a year and we lived with irreconcilable differences for another four. I make no apologies for visiting an attractive woman."

"Four years is a long time to suffer."

"I'm an optimist," I said. "I kept thinking our life would get better."

I shared with Rose that our marriage had begun with great promise. We were both in the antiquarian book trade, and I wanted nothing more than to love her and be loved in return. But that was not to be and our marriage ended with near financial ruin and my complete loss of identity. There was no room in our marriage for me to be me, I told her. I had lost who I was and what was important to me.

Rose asked me about siblings and I told her I had a brother I didn't see often enough. She mentioned she had a daughter and granddaughters she saw occasionally. We talked about other places we had lived and found we had many in common. I had lived in West Seattle before moving to the island and so had Rose. She had been on the board of an arts organization in Seattle around the time they had funded a staged reading of a play of mine in the early 1980s.

"What was the play?" she asked.

"It's called 'The Old Guitar Player'."

"What's it about?"

"An old Spaniard who had once been a great guitarist," I said, "and now lived in the shadow of his talented father. His hands became deformed and all he could do was bang on his out-of-tune strings and mumble words."

"Sounds like a sad story."

"I saw this man most every day when I lived in Spain."

"When was this?" she asked.

"1980."

"Where in Spain were you?" she asked.

"Valencia."

"Doing what?"

"Teaching English and trying to find myself."

"How'd the search turn out?"

"My first wife and I divorced two years later."

"I guess you found something," she said.

"Not what I thought."

"What were you expecting?"

"A purpose, I guess. I was working on my first book. My wife and I were teaching English but life felt empty. I thought leaving the country might be the answer. All I learned was I would never be Spanish, and my wife and I didn't have a future."

"No future?"

"Not a future I wanted."

"I was in Valencia for a while," Rose said.

"Really?"

"France, Turkey and places in between."

"Doing what?"

"I was with a man who had business there."

"What kind of business?"

"I spent a lot of time on my own."

"Well, we might have crossed paths there," I said.

"Probably sat at the same bar," she said, "snacking on *tapas*."

"I would have bought you a cognac."

"I'm sure you did," she said.

"I would remember."

"So would I," she said.

We learned we both had lived in Los Angeles and shared a mutual interest in music.

"I was a guest for ten days of a music manager named Cohen," I said.

"Herb Cohen?" she said

"I believe so."

"I knew Herb. Frank Zappa was one of his clients."

"That's the one," I said. "I spent time with several of his clients in the 70s. Tom Waits and George Duke. I went to a movie release party for one of Frank's films."

"I was probably there" she said. "I loved Frank."

"And of course the Troubadour."

"We most likely hooked up there," she said flatly. I looked at her, waiting for a smile or a laugh, but she just sipped her wine without any change in her facial expression. "Want a tour of the Ranch?"

The three chicken coops in the center of the property were 8 by 12 feet in size, with four tiers of nesting boxes in each one. The entire chicken area was enclosed in a tall wire fence. Four apple trees in the middle of the fenced area provided some shade for the chickens. Clucking hens and aggressive roosters skittered everywhere, while Bella circled the enclosure on alert for any possible threats to "the girls," as Rose called them. She told me a family of coyotes lived in the surrounding woods and were constantly looking for food and water. Occasionally a hen would get outside the fence and the next day Rose would find a clump of blood-stained feathers marking the scene of the crime. Hawks and eagles were the other big threats, she said. Rose pointed out a cloth mesh she had recently installed over the open areas around the coops to provide additional protection from above. But Bella's primary job was to protect the chickens from predators, and from what I could see, she was constantly on duty.

Rose pointed out the four roosters who ran the roost and were the most colorful.

"That one with the red around his beak," she said, "that's 'the Earl'. He's the most handsome and gets his way with the ladies."

"Tough job."

"Welcome to Jurassic Park. They're all such dinosaurs. Dumbest creatures on Earth, but I love them."

We walked back toward the house passed an old Dodge Dart sitting on blocks behind the barn.

"My deceased husband milled lumber in there," she said, "but all the equipment has been sold off. I haven't decided what to do with the barn yet."

The sun dropped down behind the trees, and the evening air took on a chill. We went back onto the rear deck again where it was still warm and protected from the evening breeze.

"How long have you lived on the island?" I asked.

"Six years."

"And West Seattle before that?"

"Just up from the Fauntleroy ferry," she said. "I lived three minutes from the ferry."

"Lincoln Park was my backyard," she said.

"Mine too," I said.

"I'm sure we crossed paths there."

"I would have tipped my hat."

"I would have consulted the Tarot."

She re-lit the pipe and handed it to me. The air was sweet from the last of the roses around the deck and the recently mowed grass. The back deck was so quiet I could hear small creatures rustling through the tall grass at the edge of the lawn. For a moment I forgot where I was and was drawn into the stillness. I looked over at Rose who appeared so at ease and peaceful.

"This has been fun," she said, "but I have baking to finish."

I drank the last of my wine. "Would you go out with me tomorrow?" I said.

She looked at me with a startled face. "Like a date?"

"Call it what you like. I just want to see you again."

She took the pipe back, re-lit the bowl, and sat back in her chair. She looked out into the trees that lined the property, and the longer she was quiet the more I was prepared to be dismissed again.

"Remember," I said, "I bruise easily."

She continued to look off into the trees, and I was getting nervous.

"I can't go out until I put the girls away," she finally said. "Come by after seven."

Chapter Five

"I JUST WANT A WEIRD AND PASSIONATE LIFE FULL OF MUSIC, ADVENTURES, UNFORGETTABLE KISSES AND GOOD CONVERSATIONS WITH STRANGE PEOPLE."
- BROOKE HAMPTON

It had been my belief if I was meant to know someone, they would come into my life without me forcing the issue. But for some unknown reason, I felt compelled to follow up on my first meeting with Rose; after our two-hour conversation at the Ranch, I still felt there was more to know. I felt Rose had something important I needed to discover and for me to find out what it was, I would have to step outside my comfort zone.

Comfort zones are called that for a reason. They are safe places where we feel good, where we're at ease and in control of our environment. Uncertainty and vulnerability are minimized. My comfort zone contained no friction, no fighting, no belittling remarks, or challenges to my manhood. I was secure in knowing who I was and what made me happy, and for the first time in many years I felt comfortable with myself. Yet I felt drawn to leave that familiar place for uncharted territory again.

That Saturday night I returned to the Ranch at 7:15 pm. Bella greeted me with a nuzzle between my legs as I knocked on the front door. When the door opened I was stunned speechless. Gone were the jeans, the bulky sweater and the heavy rubber boots. Instead Rose invited me in wearing a tight-fitting red dress that accentuated her youthful body and her beautiful legs. She looked like a forty-year old model in a Nordstrom catalog.

"Damn," I said, "you look...beautiful."

"Thank you," she said. "I haven't worn this in a long time."

Rose had the glow of a young girl on her first date, and she radiated a beauty I had not seen the day before. Her eyes glimmered with light as if reading on my face how stunning she looked. We sat down at the tall dining table in the kitchen area and she took a wine glass from the cupboard, filled my glass and topped hers off.

"So how was your day?" she asked.

"Sold a few books," I said, "and thought a lot about this chicken wrangler I just met. And yours?"

"I baked brownies and delivered six dozen eggs to another market on the island."

I couldn't take my eyes off Rose. She had such a classic beauty with none of the usual signs of time and wear that it was hard to believe we were the same age. Her natural brown hair was again wrapped up on her head and her brown eyes drew me into them with their softness. Whenever she looked at me it was as if she saw deep inside me and quietly sized up what she discovered there. The look in her eyes was both unnerving and flattering.

Suddenly the phone rang, but Rose didn't get up.

"Do you need to get that?" I said.

"If it's important, they'll leave a message."

The phone stopped ringing and went to the answering machine.

"You've reached the Ranch," Rose's soft, inviting voice rang out. "Please leave a message. I'd love to hear your voice."

"It's Marian," came a familiar voice.

"Sure you don't want to pickup?" I said.

"Just checking in," Marian said. "Call me."

"I'll call her later, "Rose said. "So, what's the plan?"

Ott & Murphy Wine Cabaret was the only live music venue in Langley, and it was a very comfortable place to have a glass of wine, socialize and hear live music. A local Gypsy jazz trio was playing that night, and the main room was full when we arrived. The only available seating was in the library area which consisted of four leather chairs surrounded by bookcases opposite the small bar.

I spent a lot of time at the wine shop on the weekends and had gotten to know the servers and the owners quite well. I performed there every other month and it had become something of a second home for me since my separation.

I ordered two glasses of Double Bluff, and we settled into the library.

"It's hard to believe how small this place was," I said, "before they expanded into the adjoining space."

"It was just this side?"

"Sat maybe 15 people."

"And you played here."

"Right where we're sitting. They moved these chairs out and two players could fit in here."

"Who did you play with?"

"Sometimes by myself," I said, "and a few times with David Ossman of The Firesign Theater. He told stories and read poems and I sang songs."

Sabra brought our drinks over, and I introduced her to Rose.

"Hey girlfriend," Rose said.

Sabra was a vibrant young woman in her thirties with several ear and eyebrow piercings, tattoos, and a spirited personality. "I like your dress," she said.

"Your tattoo is unusual," Rose said, taking hold of Sabra's forearm.

"It's not finished," Sabra said. "Still needs a little work."

"Is it a saying?" Rose asked. "I can't see without my glasses."

"It's for my father," Sabra said.

"What's he think of it?"

"He passed away. That's why it's for him,"

"Well, it's nice you remember him."

Sabra thanked her and returned to her customers at the bar. I turned to Rose.

"You have one of those?" I asked.

"I bet you would like to know," Rose said.

"I would," I said. "That's why I asked."

"Are they a problem for you?"

"Not at all," I said. "It's not something I would do, but I don't have a problem with others expressing themselves."

"Some of them are quite beautiful and ornate," she said, "and others mysterious. Like your friend's."

"I just never felt the need to paint my body," I said. "I prefer to put ink on paper."

"Maybe you're not working through anything," she said.

"We're all working through something at some time."

"For some it can be an experience they need to process," she said, "or maybe a symbol for something they can't explain in words."

"I don't have a problem with words," I said.

"Some people do," she said, "when it comes to something lost or missing."

"Perhaps," I said.

"If everybody's looking for something," she said, "what are you looking for?"

"Right now?"

"We can start there."

"I'm looking to know you better," I said.

"Not very original," she said, "but a start."

"You didn't answer my question. Do you have a tattoo?"

"You'll just have to find out for yourself."

We talked through our glass of wine as people came and went. Some people were waiting for a table at the restaurant across the street while others came in after dinner to catch some of the music. Rose's question about what I was looking for caught me off guard and when she excused herself to the restroom, I thought about her question more. I did want to know more about her, but I knew I wanted more than that. I didn't want things; what I wanted couldn't be bought in a shop or inked on my arm.

In the last two years, I had survived a chronic form of leukemia and left a marriage that had emasculated me and moved into a small apartment in town. I had lost track of who I was, and after our separation, my biggest challenge was to find myself again. My belief in a loving mate had been shattered, broken into a thousand pieces, and I was not happy with that realization. I was ready to move forward and find what life still held for me, with or without anyone else in it. Despite the turmoil in my life, the future felt strangely full of promise. I just wasn't clear what it would look like. Rose's question about what I was looking for was a much deeper issue than I could answer on the fly.

But the bigger question I faced was what had I made of my life? I had written some books, but I hadn't changed anyone's life or made a difference in any field. I was good at selling books and a fair guitar player with a voice that wasn't going to change the music world. I had written a few good songs, but most people were never going to hear them.

I reluctantly spent three and a half years in the army and did my best to be a good mate to three women. But nothing of what I had done felt like it was enough. My life felt like it was running out, at least a life that would be shared with someone else. All I had to show for it was a string of unsustained relationships and a lot of uncertainty as to what my life added up to. Little did I know the most rewarding and challenging relationship of my life was about to unfold.

Around nine, the bass player in my blues band and several of his friends came into the wine shop. They huddled around us in the library area, looking for a place to sit and I introduced Rose around. My bass player turned to Rose and asked, "So what are you two up to tonight?"

I raised my glass and nodded toward Rose. Rose, without skipping a beat, said: "I'm going to bang the beejesus out of him tonight."

Her provocative response took me completely by surprise. She didn't bat an eye or back away from her statement. The people around us went quiet as if they were deciding whether to be offended or amused. I looked at Rose searching for a clue to the validity of her statement, but all she did was smile and sip at her wine.

"Who says romance is dead," I said.

Suddenly someone laughed and everyone went back to their conversations.

We ordered another glass of wine and listened to the first song of the trio's second set. I had not eaten anything since lunch and the wine and herb were catching up with me.

I had no idea how honest Rose's announcement was, but it made me feel good in a small way that she said what she did in front of people I knew. Most everyone in town knew of my separation and the impending divorce, and it had been a while since anyone had seen me out with a woman. The more I thought about what she had publicly announced, the more concerned I was she said it as a joke, a brash statement to shock what she may have deemed an otherwise dull crowd.

"Feel like a cigarette?" I asked.

"Sure."

We stepped outside and stood in the doorway of the neighboring gem shop. I lit her cigarette then mine.

"Have I told you how beautiful you look in that dress?"

"Yes," she said, "and I saw it in your eyes at the house."

"Well, let me say it again. You are gorgeous."

She leaned over and kissed me and I pulled her close to me. The touch of her body against mine made the hair on my arms stand up, and I pressed her closer.

"I can feel I have your attention," she said.

"More than you know."

"I know."

"You certainly know how to start a conversation," I said. "Tongues will be wagging for days."

"Small towns need a spark sometimes, don't you think?"

"And you're that spark?"

"I do what I feel like doing," she said. "It's all about me."

"Everything is about you?"

"Everything that is important," she said.

"That's an interesting perspective," I said.

"I don't know about interesting," she said. "Just honest."

"Most people aren't that honest," I said. "How long have you held that position?"

"Ever since I've been on my own," she said.

"So if everything is all about you, how much room does that leave for someone else?"

"As much as I need," she said.

I leaned in and kissed her again.

"Let's pay up," she said, "and go to your place."

Chapter Six

"A LADY DOESN'T WALK WITH A CIGARETTE."
- ROSE

From Ott & Murphy, it was a three-minute walk to my street level apartment in a house on 2nd Street. Langley is a small seaside village forty-five minutes north of Seattle with a population of a thousand souls. The town has three commercial streets filled with unique retail shops, including my rare book shop, art galleries, restaurants, charming inns, and the small Clyde movie theater.

Normally the streets of Langley rolled up by 9 p.m., but once we left the wine shop we found ourselves engulfed with people exiting the theater. I could feel Rose's hand tighten up as we made our way through the crowd and I offered her a cigarette.

"A lady doesn't walk with a cigarette," she said.

Her sudden sense of propriety took me by surprise. She could tell a group of strangers she planned to bang the daylights out of me, but not walk in public with a cigarette. The longer I was around Rose, the more intrigued I became by her unique code of behavior. Her pronouncements were often provocative and at times shocking, but there was a freshness to her I was drawn to. Her blunt responses and candid observations were new to me and reflected a radical approach to the art of conversation.

Whidbey Island has a special attraction, especially the south end. The island's appeal has nothing to do with industry or high paying jobs. Whidbey Island's magical allure attracts not only creatives of broad and diverse disciplines, but those with a deep spiritual connection the island seems to foster. No one is transferred to South Whidbey; a great many residents were drawn to the island's growing Bohemian community back in the 1970s, its rural life, the silent rhythm of the swirling waters that surround the island or the unseen magnetism locked deep in the soil. Still others move to the island to retire, a few because they get romantically involved with an islander, and others to heal from a painful past. Ironically my first wife moved to the island not long after we divorced. Some people come to the island to escape a previous life and start fresh. For me it was my soon to be ex-wife who drew me to the island but, even though that life was over, I had no desire to leave. The island's magic had gotten under my skin, and I couldn't imagine a better place to live. And now Rose had suddenly gotten my attention, and I was drawn to her like an iron chip to a magnet.

My apartment was warm and Rose immediately took off her coat and draped it over the back of my couch. I went into the kitchen and pulled a bottle of wine off the shelf. Rose sat down on one of the two stools at the kitchen counter.

"Are you always as outspoken as you were in the wine shop?" I asked, from the kitchen.

"Did it bother you?"

"I don't know about bothered so much as it surprised me."

"I just said what I felt," she said.

"What are you feeling right now?"

"Do you really want to know?"

"I think so."

"Can we smoke?"

"Not in here," I said, "but we can sit outside."

She draped her coat over her shoulders, grabbed her glass of wine and we sat outside on the L-shaped bench. It was a clear, beautiful night, and there were happy voices echoing from the outside deck of the pub across the street. Rose took a small pipe from her pocket and lit up. We sat there quietly listening to the voices at the pub, people we could hear but not see because of the foliage that gave my little porch area privacy. Suddenly Rose got up, stepped in front of me, spread my legs apart and straddled my right leg.

"Am I too heavy?"

"Not at all."

"Good." She leaned forward and kissed me. This time it was a long, passionate kiss. She slowly rocked as I pulled her close to me. Her movements got more intense as did her breathing and my heart started to pound. Then as quickly as she had mounted my leg, she stood up, adjusted her dress and sat back down on the bench. We finished the pipe and went back inside. I was still aroused by her straddling my leg and the effect her soft lips had on mine. I pulled the door shut and drew the heavy drapes closed behind me.

I went into the kitchen for more wine and Rose stood next to the dining table leaning against the back of my couch. Maybe it was the wine and the smoke, but she looked even more stunning than earlier in the evening. I stood opposite her and just stared at her as she looked at me like she was sizing me up. She sipped her wine and finally broke the silence between us.

"Take off your clothes," she said.

"Excuse me?"

She said it so matter-of-factly I just looked at her waiting for a sign she was making a joke. We were standing in the middle of my dining area, holding our glasses of wine with all the lights on. I couldn't think of a more uncomfortable request. I wasn't twenty-five and the thought of taking off my clothes at my age in front of a woman I hardly knew, under bright lights just felt wrong. Once again, my comfort zone was being challenged.

"Come on," she said. "Take them off."

"This is a joke, right?"

"I want to see you."

"What makes you think I'm that easy."

"We'll find out."

"You first then," I said.

"Alright," she said.

She set her wine glass down and slowly unzipped the back of her red dress. I slowly unbuttoned my shirt as she slipped out of her dress, exposing her red bra and matching lacey boy-panties. I threw my shirt on the chair next to me, unbuckled my pants and pulled them off. She undid her bra revealing her firm breasts then gracefully removed her panties. I slipped out of my shorts and for a moment we stood there, four feet apart, just looking at each other. She leaned against the back of the couch and sipped her wine. She looked so casual and relaxed as though she were posing for a Playboy photo.

I had never felt more exposed as I did right then. There were no physical secrets between us. Everything was right there in the open…unfettered and unadorned.

As I looked at Rose's body, I did not see a woman in her sixties. There didn't appear to be an ounce of extra weight on her small frame. I, on the other hand, could have easily lost twenty pounds, and I suddenly felt as though the evening would end at any moment. The longer I looked at her, the more my body responded to seeing her absolutely beautiful body.

"You are so cute and hunky," she said.

"And you are a knockout."

I was relieved at her assessment, yet fully prepared for her to put her clothes back on and call it a night. I slowly approached her and kissed her. She wrapped her arms around me and pulled me closer. I felt myself respond to her touch. She stood up straight so she could feel me against her, then reached down, took me in her hand, and gently rubbed me against her body.

"Let's take this to the bed," I whispered.

"Are you sure?" she said.

"I'm positive."

"Really sure?"

"Painfully sure."

For the next hour we rolled and tumbled, stroked and rubbed each other, in an exploratory exercise of tactile pleasure. Her skin was soft to my lips and everywhere I kissed her triggered the most soulful sounds of pleasure. I rolled her over onto her stomach and gently pressed my fingers up and down her back, over her perfectly round bum, then down her slender legs and back up again to her neck. When I entered her, I felt enveloped in a velvet sheath perfectly molded to me. We remained engaged through multiple positions until we both finally collapsed out of exhaustion. We just lay next to each other in a tender embrace, but between the wine and the anticipation all we could do was laugh at what had not happened.

"Did we have fun?" she whispered.

"I believe so."

"It felt like we did," she said.

"It was good," I said. "It's just been a while."

"I was afraid I was dried up."

"You were fine," I said.

She kissed my cheek then sat up. "I have to go."

"Can't you stay? We could try again."

"I can't tonight. Bella will be worried."

"And I'll miss you."

"You'll be fine."

Rose sat up on the edge of the bed, then slid off, walked to the dining area and slipped back into her clothes. I sat up and watched her zip herself up. I wanted more that night, but neither of us was physically able for more. What we had that night was more than I had expected for a first date, but I secretly hoped it hadn't ended things before we had a chance to really get started.

I got up and got dressed. During the walk back to my car and the five minute drive to the Ranch we were quiet but not to the point of being uncomfortable —more like contemplation at least on my part. I couldn't stop thinking about how brazen Rose had been at the wine shop and the whole getting naked followed by all the wonderful sensations we shared in bed. And while the evening didn't end perfectly, intense pleasure had been shared and an obvious level of comfort had been reached that more than made up for our inability to completely consummate the evening.

When we got to the Ranch, I got out of the car and went around and opened her door and took her hand.

"He'p me," she said, as I lifted her out of my low-riding car. "He'p me."

"I had a great time tonight," I said.

"Me too."

"You're not just saying that, are you?"

"It was fun and you should come over for dinner Monday."

"I can do that," I said. I kissed her and once again my body responded immediately.

"Keep that where it is," she said. "We've had enough for one night. Good night."

And with those parting words, I watched Rose climb the front stairs. I waited until she went inside then got back in my car. She waved through the glass door, and then turned off the porch light.

Chapter Seven

"WHO SAID ANY OF THIS IS FAIR."
- ROSE

Focusing on book selling was hard after my first date with Rose. I did my best to attend to business and not allow my mind to wander into the realm of what surprises might lie ahead. I replayed every moment over and over trying to absorb what had happened and what was said to reassure myself we were still good. The fact we were both able to laugh about our first sexual encounter eased my concern as did the fact she invited me for dinner. If there hadn't been a connection, I was confident she would have ended everything Saturday night.

As much as I wanted to relish the weekend moments, I was still in the process of getting a divorce. Without a lawyer, I was doing everything myself which meant a lot of paperwork and documents to file. My wife and I had been separated for over a year and there had been some spiteful delays in moving the process forward. But when I finally filed the paperwork, the 90-day clock started and if all went smoothly the divorce would be final by Christmas. In the meantime, I needed to focus on selling books to cover the additional cost of the divorce.

While I was starting to feel a sense of renewal with Rose, I was also clearing the slate of my past complications so I could start over again—this time fresh. In the meantime, my heart was still hidden. After years of thwarted affection my heart had gone numb and had retreated deep into my chest. It was so encased in scar tissue I had forgotten I had a heart, and I needed to find it again.

The weekend passed quickly, and I was looking forward to my Monday night dinner date with Rose. She had a magnetism that kept pulling at me especially when we were apart. When I wasn't with her I wanted her company; and when I was with her I wanted to know as much as possible. I wanted to touch that part of her that drew me to her like a moth to a bright light.

I closed the shop at five, picked up a bottle of wine and drove over to the Ranch. The days were definitely getting shorter and there was a noticeable chill in the air. I pulled up in front of the house and again was immediately greeted by the ever-vigilant Bella. I gave her a hearty head rub and a gentle pat on her back.

"Bella needs a treat," Rose called out from the open front door.

"All I have in the car are some Altoids."

"We'll have to correct that if you're going to keep coming around," she said. "Bella's a working dog. She needs her treats."

I walked up the stairs and followed Rose inside. The house was warm and smelled of fresh garlic. Rose went to a kitchen cupboard, rustled in a bag, and came back with two dog biscuits.

"Here," she said. "She'll love you forever."

I gave Bella the biscuits which she ate with one crunch, and then she stared up at me longingly.

Rose leaned into me. "Now a dog bone from the freezer," she whispered.

"So there's a whole routine?" I whispered back.

"You bet."

I pulled open the freezer and gave Bella a bone which she immediately took into the living room.

"I hope you like meatloaf," Rose said.

"I do."

"I made it today for the market. Thought we would have the same."

"Fine with me. Anything I can do?"

"Just have a seat and keep me company."

She took the bottle of wine from me and put it in the freezer. "Can I get you something to drink?"

"Whatever you're having."

"Happy Coffee," she said.

"Sounds intriguing," I said.

"Turkish coffee and Irish Crème."

I sat at the kitchen table, opposite the refrigerator, and watched as she brewed up my coffee. The refrigerator had French doors with a bottom freezer, and there were little notes taped to the front of the doors. From where I was sitting the notes appeared to be shopping lists, items from different stores she needed for baking and for meals. To my surprise there were no pictures or photographs. No grandchildren, no daughter, or loved ones or old friends. No images of her deceased husband to take her back to some other time or place or memory.

I wondered what kind of man her husband was. Not so much what he did for a living, but how he treated Rose? Was he a lover, a passionate man who appreciated her beauty? Were they madly in love? Was Rose as bold with him as she had been with me?

I remembered how she glowed when I responded to her red dress and that she said she hadn't worn it in a while. I wondered how much they loved each other, and was he as intriguing as Rose?

"So tell me about your market?" I asked.

"I do baked goods and obviously fresh eggs," she said. "During the week I make up small dinners people can take home and heat up. I also have an Alzheimer's couple I cook for. I make them a week's worth of meals every Thursday."

"And the market does well?"

"Well enough. It's steady money. It's hard sometimes to have enough eggs. People love my eggs. They're all natural and people can taste the difference. How's the book world?"

"Some days are better than others but overall business is good. I also work part time as a checker at the Red Apple."

"Why?"

"Old debts," I said, "but I've realized I'm not built to work for someone else."

"I worked for a computer company for a while," she said, "but I prefer being my own boss." She checked on dinner and set her timer. "It'll be another thirty minutes for the potatoes."

She delivered our coffees then sat down at the kitchen table.

"This is very tasty," I said.

"You can have something stronger if you want. I have some Vodka and I think some Tequila."

"After the other night, I'll stick with this for now."

"So," she said, sitting back in her chair. "…did we actually…you know…the other night?"

"Well, we did but…."

"Oh shit, did I do something embarrassing?"

"No. I mean we did, but I'm not sure it was completely consummated."

"I remember feeling good when I got home," she said.

"It was all good, but it didn't feel like we got anywhere."

"I was nervous," she said. "It's been awhile."

"Me too."

She stared at me with the intensity of someone trying to decide something important. She leaned forward in her chair and smiled. "You are cute and hunky," she said.

That was the second time she had referred to me as cute and hunky and, as pleasant as it sounded, I was confused by the reference. I never thought of myself as cute, at least not for the last forty years, and I had no idea what "hunky" meant.

"I remember that about you," she said.

"Before or after we got naked in my dining room?"

"We did that?" she said. "I wasn't sure that really happened."

"It did and you have the sexiest body I've ever seen."

"For an old broad."

"For any broad."

She slowly slid off her chair, walked over to me, and kissed me long and hard. I pulled her closer to me and the kiss got even more intense. Then just as quickly as she came to me, she broke off the kiss and went back to her chair.

"That's so unfair," I said.

"Who says any of this is fair." She walked to the oven, checked the potatoes, and took some greens out of the refrigerator.

"So how long has it been?" I asked.

"For what?"

"Since your husband died."

"About seven months."

"I'm sorry."

"You do like salad, don't you?"

"Sure," I said. "I didn't mean to pry. Marian mentioned what had happened."

"It's okay. So how long were you married?"

"Ten years," I said.

"That's a long time."

"A few of them were better than the rest."

"And now you're leaving," she said.

"We both left a while ago," I said. "It had not been good for either of us."

I explained to Rose we had started out with great promise. We were both in the bookselling trade and that should have made for a solid foundation for us. But personalities came into play and we slowly devolved to the point where neither of us liked the other.

"Bottom line is," I said, "we were opposites."

"Aren't they suppose to attract?"

"But not always sustain," I said. "You can only go so long not wanting to be around your mate before you realize the marriage is toxic. And you? How long were you married?"

"Bob and I were together six years," she said, "but married for a week before he died."

"A week," I said, "after being together all those years?"

"Ironic, isn't it?"

"What happened?"

"Aortic aneurism. He died in bed."

"Were you…?"

"No," she said. "He just died in bed. And since you separated?"

"What do you mean?"

"How many women?"

"This was not about other women."

"Okay."

"I did have a date last Valentine's Day, but that didn't go anywhere."

The kitchen timer went off and Rose got up and prepared our plates then brought them to the table.

"Bon appetite," she said

Rose was a good cook, but to look around at her home you would have never known of her talents. To the unknowing eye, the rustic nature of the house would overshadow her skills and the warmth that filled the house. The house was lived in, not a staged photo for a Better Homes and Gardens spread. Where we live says a lot about who we are. It reflects our basic nature. The house was simple and functional, and the beauty of it resided in the woman who lived in it. Like the house, Rose was unpretentious and earthy. Nothing was forced or extraneous to her needs. To me, it felt like a real home: It was warm and furnished for utility.

The meat loaf was tasty, and everything about our dinner date was perfect especially the easy conversation. I was interested in her time in Los Angeles in the 70s, which was when I lived there. She told me she had spent time in an apartment connected to the singer Jackson Browne when he was just getting started. She said he would play the same piano riff over and over to the point of driving her out. Eventually the riff became one of Browne's best known songs, but to this day, she said, whenever she hears that song on the radio she wants to run away.

I told her I was a big David Crosby fan, especially his first solo album. She had nothing good to say about him based on personal experience. She didn't elaborate, and I didn't ask. We both agreed that Lowell George was a special talent and his band Little Feat a great group. I told her about the writing I had done and that I had three published books.

"I started the first one when I moved to Spain," I said.

"Why Spain?"

"I wanted to live some place far away and foreign," I said.

"Somebody chasing you?"

"Let's just say I didn't feel at home here. When I got discharged from the army, everything back home felt foreign, like I didn't belong anymore. After I got my degree my first wife and I moved to L.A. but that wasn't home either. I needed to go somewhere foreign. I liked the Latin culture and Spain seemed far enough away."

"And foreign."

"Foreign enough. But things fell apart there too," I said.

"In what way?"

I explained the couple we were supposed to share a large apartment with in Valencia had split up just before we got there. The guy kept the apartment, and his wife moved in with a friend. One of the three bedrooms in the large apartment had been rented to a young Chilean and we got the remaining room. By the time we arrived in Valencia, Spain was already broken for us.

"But you started your first book there," Rose said.

"I found myself trying to remember my life before I felt lost."

I told Rose that within six months my wife and I would leave Spain and two years later get divorced.

"Earlier, you mentioned Herb Cohen," she said.

"I did," I said. "I wrote about music for the university daily newspaper and Herb got me two days with Tom Waits, an invite to Stevie Wonder's birthday party and into the press party for one of Zappa's movies."

"Frank was one of the true artists in L.A.," she said. "He was a real gentleman and I loved his wife."

"I just spoke with Frank briefly," I said, "but I liked him immediately."

"My first husband played with Frank," she said, "and I sang a little backup."

"I'm impressed," I said. "Rock royalty."

"I was probably at Frank's movie release," she said.

"Wouldn't that be something," I said. "It was in a luxury hotel suite with a lot of beautiful people there."

"We probably hooked up that night."

"Entirely possible," I countered.

"I'm sure we did," she said. "I would have taken you in a minute."

"I would not have forgotten that."

We finished dinner and, after Rose cleared our dishes, she put a plate with two cupcakes in front of me.

"You should taste my wares," she said.

"I believe I already have," I said,

"Don't go there," she said.

"But I'll gladly try one of your cupcakes."

"It's chilling down," she said. "Would you start a fire while I clean up?"

Once I got the fire up and roaring, I perused a tall glass display case Rose had in her dining room. The case was filled with several scrimshaw items; a knife with an elaborately carved whale bone handle, some fine glassware, and native Alaskan artifacts including handmade fishhooks made out of bone. I looked around for other personal treasures and immediately realized there were no photographs in frames on her wooden desk or on the walls. No childhood snapshots, nothing in the way of reminders of past times, glory days, or special moments to remember. I thought of the one photograph I had in my apartment; it was of my father, my brother and me taken a few years before my father passed away. For some reason, the words "balance disrupted" came to mind.

Rose finished washing our dishes and was putting away the leftovers when she asked what I did at the Chamber of Commerce.

"Actually I'm the president right now." I walked back into the kitchen.

"Oh wow. A politico."

"Politico with a small 'p'. But you can call me *El Presidente*."

"Well *El Presidente*, how do you like it?"

"I'm not good with group think."

"Me neither," she said. "I know what's best for me, and I do me the best."

We sat at the kitchen table enjoying the warmth of the fire. There was a pause in the conversation where we just looked at each other. Rose turned away and smiled when she saw me staring at her. There was a child-like innocence to her at times that made her even more adorable. She had an ease to her that made talking effortless without anything feeling forced, and it was hard to take my eyes off her. I loved the velvet beret she wore over her hair and her compact body that made me want to wrap my arms around her and never let go.

Finally she looked back at me, looking at her without any words being spoken, and I could feel the attraction between us like we felt the heat from the stove.

"You are so cute," she said. She slid off her chair, straddled my right leg, and kissed me hard.

"Come on," she said, and she pulled me off my chair. She led me to the rear of the house and a small bedroom with a huge California King size bed.

That night we made up for what had not happened the first time we were intimate. As anxious as she had been to get into bed, she was calm and completely relaxed once we touched and held each other. We were in no hurry to get anywhere except close to each other. The more we explored, the deeper the experience we shared. Suddenly, she broke off her kiss.

"Have you found it yet?" she whispered.

"What am I looking for?" I whispered back.

"You asked about a tattoo," she said.

"It's a little dark for that," I said.

"I have faith in you."

I ran my hand over her face, down her soft neck, and gently kissed her full breasts while I discreetly looked for any sign of a tattoo. I lightly squeezed her nipples, and Rose immediately responded to my touch. I slowly drew my fingers down her flat stomach then cupped my hand between her legs. She shivered at my touch and my gentle probing and, when I slowly slid down, she opened her legs wider and I lightly kissed her. The longer I kissed her, the faster her breathing got until she finally stiffened and writhed with repeated waves of pleasure. I continued to lightly kiss her until she pulled me away.

"Stop," she said, breathing deeply. "No more. You're trying to kill me."

I moved up next to her and held her in my arms while she caught her breath. Her pleasure made me feel good. If nothing else happened, at least she had been pleased and the intimacy demons that had plagued my marriage were not at the Ranch.

"Are you alright?" I asked.

"I'm fine," she said, as she tried to catch her breath.

"I wasn't trying to kill you."

"I have heart issues," she said. "It just got very intense."

"What kind of issues?"

She sat up and took a drink of water. "Ten years ago I had a heart attack, in Costco of all places. I should have died. Actually I was dead for a while."

"And now?"

"I take medication."

"I didn't know. Are you sure you're okay?"

"I'm fine," she said, "but at times I feel like I'm living on borrowed time." She slid back into bed, reached under the blanket, and took me in her hand. She gently slid me inside her and began slowly moving her hips. She kissed me and dragged her nails along the inside of my thighs until I finished and collapsed next to her.

For the first time in years, I felt totally relaxed and at ease with the woman in bed next to me. I held her close to me and the softness of her skin was like the silky part of a baby's blanket. All I could think about was how happy I was, and I didn't want the feeling to end.

Rose got out of bed and slipped on her jeans and a sweater. "I have to put the chickens away," she said abruptly.

"Well, now that you've had your way with me," I said, "I'm being tossed aside for chickens."

"Dinosaurs," she said.

"I'm crushed."

"You'll survive."

"I'm not so sure. First the empty beer bottles and now the chickens."

"You'll be fine."

"Only if I can see you again."

"You will," she said.

I got dressed, collected my coat and hat, and followed her into the kitchen. She took a zip-lock bag out of a drawer, reached into a bag under the spice rack, and then handed me the plastic bag.

"What's this?" I said.

"Bella treats," she said. "You'll need these when you come over."

She opened the kitchen door and stepped out onto the landing. She slipped on her rubber boots and grabbed a flashlight.

"Thanks for dinner," I said, as we walked toward my car, "and…dessert. It was nice."

"Oh *thank you El Presidente*. The pleasure was all mine."

Chapter Eight

"How do you like these?"
- Rose

I'm sure I fell in love with Rose the day I first visited her at the Ranch. Since that day, her devil-may-care attitude drew me even closer to her and I was intrigued that I couldn't stop thinking about her. I had never experienced such a strong attraction on so many levels as I felt with Rose. I also had the strongest feeling I had known her previously. Sometimes you just know when someone strikes you as familiar in a way that is beyond any rational explanation. She felt important in my life, but I wasn't sure how or why. Clearly, I didn't know all there was to know about Rose. But she had such a calm about her I couldn't imagine anyone more comfortable with themselves. She was self-assured and playful and a bit mysterious. Not mysterious in a mystical way; it had more to do with what she didn't say which left me wanting to know more.

The things people don't talk about in their life are often issues of the deepest concern. Those subjects can be avoided, glossed over, or given cursory attention, but more often than not, the things people don't talk about say more about them than the things they do say. And I wondered about the things Rose left unsaid.

Rose was not someone who talked just to fill the air with sound. She was comfortable with quiet, and spoke when she had something to say or a question she needed answering.

She was also age-appropriate. What I had always found attractive in some younger women was their freshness, their sense of fun, their youthful beauty, their firm bodies, and their enthusiasm as lovers. Rose had all those attributes and more. The one thing missing with a much younger woman is the generational connection. The shared experiences: the historical events you have in common as well as the cultural references you share.

Over the next few days, I re-focused myself on selling books and preparing for an upcoming music performance in town. But Rose was always on my mind. We had left things open, and I didn't want to press her too hard.

A few nights after our dinner date, I went home after work and put in some guitar work. I practiced wearing headphones so I wouldn't disturb my landlady upstairs. I could play as loud as I wanted without bothering anyone else. I was playing along with my loop machine when I felt someone looking in at me. I looked up and saw Rose standing outside my door smiling in at me. I pulled off my headphones and went to the door.

"Hey you," I said, when I opened the door.

"I didn't want to knock and disturb you," she said. "You looked very focused."

"Just putting in some practice time," I said.

"Can we sit outside?" she said.

"Sure. A glass of wine?"

I grabbed an open bottle, two glasses, and sat down next to her on the outside bench. The night air was cool, and she kept her coat on.

"To what do I owe this unexpected visit?"

"I felt like seeing you."

"I'm glad you feel that way," I said. "I've thought about you a lot since the other night."

"Is that so?"

"It is so," I said. "You're a great cook and an even better lover."

"You weren't so bad yourself…*El Presidente*."

She leaned over and kissed me. Her lips were soft and moist, and the way she gently cupped my face in her hands was comforting. She crawled onto my lap and pulled me close. Then she abruptly broke off the kiss and, as we looked at each other, she slipped off her coat.

"You are very hunky...*El Presidente*."

"And I like you too."

She grabbed the hem of her sweater and slowly raised it to expose her bare breasts. "How do you like these?"

"Very much," I said. "They're beautiful."

She kissed me again and I gently touched her breasts as she wrapped her arms around my neck.

"Let's take this inside," I said.

"No," she said, "just kiss me."

I kissed her and took her breasts in my hands.

"Look at me," she said.

I looked straight into her eyes.

"What do you see?"

"The most beautiful woman in the world."

"No. What do you really see?"

My mind raced trying to assess what I truly saw. I wasn't sure what she was looking for in a response, but I quickly felt in a difficult position. Was she looking for flattery or some deep insight into the human condition?

"Fragile desire?" I said finally.

"I want you to really want me," she said.

"Trust me," I said, "I do."

She pulled her sweater down, gently eased my hands out from under it and sat back down on the bench.

"You can't do this to me."

"You're a big boy."

"Then why did you come over?"

"To see you, and have you see me," she said.

"And get me all wired up?"

"Rub one out if you need to," she said, as she sipped her wine.

"Is that what you're going to do?"

"It's what I did before I came over here."

"This is too much," I said. "You're killing me."

"I thought of you while I did it," she said, "if that makes you feel better."

"I don't believe this," I said.

She slipped her coat back on and stood up. "I have to go." She cupped my face again and kissed me. "You're so cute when you're horny."

"And you're leaving me like this?"

"I'm coming to see you play Saturday night. Be on your best behavior," she said. "You might get lucky." With that, she walked out the driveway to her car and, as quickly as she had come to me, she went right back into the dark.

Chapter Nine

"Just call it what it is..."
- Rose

The two focuses in my life on the island were selling books and making music: one provided me a living, the other fed my soul. The blues is my music of choice, with its universal truths played within a series of simple chord progressions. The frame work of the blues allows for any number of interpretations whether it is tempo, phrasing of lyrics, or the qualities of the singer's voice that allows room to experiment and get creative within a specific format. There is so much that can be done with one, two or three chords depending on what is said and how it is presented. John Lee Hooker not only made a musical career off one-chord songs he also created a number of classic songs that have been covered by just about everyone. For me, the blues was the perfect platform for the music I wanted to play and write, and it suited my gravelly voice.

With the blues, its simplicity gets to the truth of life. The longer we are alive the more we seek the simple truths: the verity of love and pain and loss along with the struggle to live another day. And I felt Rose got what was important in my life. She repeatedly referenced my blues opera whenever I talked about writing songs and telling stories.

Rose had a sixth sense about music. She had clearly been around a lot of great musicians, and she enjoyed playing me recordings of groups I had not heard before. She had a preference for southern roots music with an emphasis on bands out of Louisiana. Many of the sounds were new to me, and there were rhythms and instrumentations I found intriguing. On the weekends, we listened to the local blues program on the radio as we talked or tended to her market tasks. Suddenly Rose would hear something in a song that would send her dancing around the kitchen. She would turn to me and say: “You could do this.” It made me smile to have her pay that much attention to what I enjoyed doing and going out of her way to expose me to new forms of expression. She knew music and knew enough about me and my interests to broaden my knowledge.

Saturday night my trio started our Ott & Murphy gig right at 7 p.m. and twenty minutes into the first set the front door opened and I saw a group of women come in. I immediately recognized Rose's signature bandana and the evening suddenly got better for me. She and her girlfriends took a table at the rear of the small room and for me the energy level in the room raised dramatically.

We played out the rest of the first set and took a short break. I went straight to the back of the room and greeted Rose with a quick kiss.

"Hey," Rose said. "You guys sound great."

"Good to see you here tonight."

"I said you might get lucky."

"Lucky I am," I said.

"These are my neighbors Rozie and Kennedy," she said. Marian stood and greeted me with a hug.

"I'm stepping outside for a moment," I said to Rose. "Join me?"

"Sure," she said.

We went outside and stood inside the covered doorway of the neighboring gem shop.

"You guys really do sound good in there."

"I wasn't sure I'd see you tonight."

"I wanted to get the girls together and bring you a crowd."

I leaned in and kissed her. "I've missed you this week."

"Well, here I am."

I kissed her again. "So what sort of surprise do you have for me tonight?"

"What do you mean, *El Presidente*?"

"Planning on making any public announcements tonight concerning our love life or exposing any lady parts?"

"I have no idea what you're talking about."

"Well, whatever you do, don't leave tonight."

"I wasn't planning on it," she said. "You're driving me home."

Our second set was especially enthusiastic, in part because Rose was in the house and I always put extra effort into a performance when I'm playing to someone special. I wanted her to hear me at my best, and I wanted her to like what I did. We finished off the night with a Texas barrelhouse number called "Jacksboro Highway" written by an old friend of mine. It took me a half hour to break down my gear and by then Rose's friends had left, and she was waiting for me at the bar.

"Hey sailor," she said, when I approached her. "Take a gal for a ride?"

When we got to the Ranch, I walked around the car and opened the door for Rose. “He’p me,” she said, “he’p me.” I took her by the hand and lifted her out. I grabbed my guitar and locked up everything else in the car.

The fire Rose had started earlier in the wood stove had burned down to a layer of hot coals. When she went into the bathroom, I fed the stove a fresh load of wood until once again it was roaring. I turned my backside to the stove and looked around for a comfortable place for us to sit and unwind. In the small living room there was a long red camelback sofa with Bella stretched out on it and adjacent the sofa was a lone upholstered armchair. Opposite the sofa there was a small Windsor rocking chair that looked like it was built for a small child. The chair felt totally out of place since there were no children in the house, and it was too small for an adult. The furniture was an odd mix. The red sofa and the arm chair didn’t feel like Rose at all. Only the Windsor chair felt feminine along with the small coffee table with its ornate wood trim and mirrored top.

Rose came into the room still in her short black skirt and black mesh stockings.

"It's nice and warm in here," she said.

"I got your fire started again."

"Thank you," she said. "Something to drink?"

"Whatever you're having."

"Why don't you pour us some wine," she said, "while I fix us a place where it's warm?"

Off the front entryway, there was an antique dining table with a centerpiece of fresh flowers on it. Rose pulled two of the dining chairs over and set them across from the stove. She grabbed the small table from next to the armchair and set it between the two dining chairs.

I brought our glasses of wine over and we sat opposite the glowing stove.

"Nice job," I said. "Very cozy."

"Here's to sounding great tonight," she said, raising her glass.

"I'm glad you came with your friends."

"Everybody thought you sounded good."

"I tend to play with more enthusiasm when I have someone to play to. If that makes sense."

"It does. Thank you again for the fire." She got up and went into the kitchen, turned down the lights, and came back with her pipe and an ashtray. We sat there with only the orange glow of the stove lighting the room and the crackling of the burning wood.

“We should see about getting your whole band to play the Rod ‘n Gun Club,” she said. “You guys would be perfect there. They’d love you.”

“That would be nice. Who do I talk to?”

“The manager, I think,” she said. “I’ll see about it.”

“The mesh stockings are a nice touch,” I said.

“Thought I’d spice up the night.”

“You’re giving me too much to think about,” I said. As exhausted as I was from two hours of singing and playing, just looking at Rose in her short dress was like a shot of adrenalin.

“I can’t imagine what it would feel like to play in front of thousands of people,” I said. “How could you come down from that rush?”

“Drugs,” she said. “But that’s where it can all go wrong. I’ve seen it too many times.”

We sat in the glow of the fire and talked about the adrenalin high you get from performing live, and how long it takes to come down from it. She faced her chair toward me and stretched her legs over mine. She inched her skirt up and started touching herself, all the time looking right into my eyes.

“Now you’re just messing with me,” I said.

“You were talking about an adrenalin high.”

“It just went into overdrive.”

“I want to see what it takes to move you.”

"Not much more of that," I said. "I want to make love to you something fierce."

"I hate that phrase," she said. "Just call it what it is."

"Okay, I want to bang you bad."

"Now doesn't that feel better?" she said.

"In my experience, most women wouldn't like that kind of directness."

"They're not me."

"Clearly."

"I believe in saying what I mean," she said. "Cutting through the bullshit. Don't talk to me about making love. Talk about banging me till next Thursday."

"Next Thursday," I said.

"Yes…next Thursday."

"Do your granddaughters know this woman across from me?"

"I'm the wild grandma who brings them even wilder clothes."

"I just don't see you as a grandma, with this unconventional side of you."

"In time I hope they'll understand this side of me."

She stopped touching herself and sat up in her chair. "I'm ready for next Thursday, *El Presidente*."

Chapter Ten

"EVERYBODY THERE HAS A STORY."
- ROSE

On one of my days off from the grocery store, Rose called me at the shop and asked if I would do her a favor and pick up some dog bones for Bella. Rose was in the middle of a baking frenzy, and Bella had worked very hard scaring off coyotes and eagles all day and she was out of treats. It was an employee crisis, Rose said, so I drove up the island and picked up enough bones for a week.

Rose had prepared dinner for us when I got to the Ranch, and the house had the wonderful smell of a chophouse.

"Lucy, I'm home," I called out from the front door.

"Hey Desi…somebody is feeling ignored."

Bella ran up to me and nuzzled between my legs.

"The coyotes were running through here today," she said. "Bella was out on the perimeter all afternoon."

"Well let's take care of that," I said. I opened one of the packages of bones and gave Bella one. "Any casualties?"

"No…but there was plenty of action."

Bella was the hardest working member of the Ranch staff. She was always on duty even when she appeared resting or was in bed at night. She was a big dog who slept on the bed with us, when I stayed over, and easily occupied half of it by herself. The slightest noise outside would wake her up, elicit a series of barks, followed by a mad dash to the front door.

Rose prepared a wonderful dinner of pork chops, garlic mashed potatoes, and a fresh green salad; it was a dinner that could have been prepared by a Main Street diner. She was also an industrious baker, which was how she kept her roadside market filled with inexpensive brownies, muffins and cupcakes. Before she moved to the island, she had her own chocolate stand in the Pike Place Market where she sold her handmade chocolates. She was very proud of her chocolate background and gave me a layman's overview of just how involved the process was to make quality truffles and other confections. She had Ganache frames and special spatulas, truffle forks for decorative designs and she explained the critical process of tempering chocolate to create a smooth, glossy coating that produced a noticeable snap when you bit into it. She clearly knew food and specialty items and had the plucky personality to market them.

After dinner, I cleared the dishes and washed them up, while Rose whipped up a batch of vanilla icing. She had baked two dozen cupcakes that afternoon and they needed to be frosted before they went up to the market. She also had several dozen eggs to clean and box up, so I volunteered to ice the cupcakes while she addressed the eggs. We turned on some Little Feat and talked while we each worked on our tasks. When I finished my icing, Rose walked over to examine my work.

"Good job," she said. She sat down across from me and took a sip of her wine. "I'm going to New Orleans in January," she said. "With Marian and her boyfriend Mike. For Mardi Gras."

"Sounds like fun," I said.

"Have you ever been?"

"Never."

She leaned forward in her chair and just looked at me for a moment. "Would you like to go?"

"You mean someday?"

"No…with us…with me."

"With you?"

There was a moment of silence between us.

"You don't have to if...," she started to say.

"Sure," I said. "It sounds great."

"I've already paid for a place to stay so that wouldn't cost you anything."

"In January?"

"We'll be there for the beginning of Mardi Gras and the Super Bowl."

"New Orleans...in January."

"You know...if it's a problem...."

"It's not a problem. You just caught me off guard."

"Well, like I said, the room is already paid for."

"I'd like that," I said. "Is this something you and Bob did?"

"Excuse me."

"You and Bob," I said. "Did the two of you go to New Orleans?"

"Bob was not a part of New Orleans," she said.

"He didn't like the town?"

"It wasn't something I wanted to do with him."

"Well... I'm flattered," I said. "I've always wanted to go there. It's a town full of history."

"And music," she said. "I think you need to experience it."

Her sudden invite caught me by surprise. I was excited and pleased she wanted me to go on vacation with her to one of the more exciting cities in the country. Her invitation said something, previously unspoken, about the state of our relationship. She clearly felt comfortable enough with me to spend five days together in a city known for its fun and party atmosphere.

"The music alone will be good for you," she said.

"Think so?" I said.

"If everybody's got a story," I said, "tell me yours."

"I've been thinking about that a lot lately," she said.

"And what did you come up with?"

"It's complicated," she said. "It has a lot of pieces."

"How many pieces are we talking about?"

"A lifetime," she said, "and many of them are good."

"And the ones that aren't?"

"You live with them," she said, "and make the most." She butted her cigarette and refilled our glasses.

Rose's invitation marked an interesting shift with us. Her comments on the stories people have to tell were intriguing even if she wasn't forthcoming about her own story. For a moment, I wondered about what she didn't talk about, then the thought of going to New Orleans and all that could unfold there replaced my momentary interest in things not said. Despite her cryptic responses, I was flattered by her invite to join her in New Orleans.

“So what do you think about New Orleans?” she said.

“Anywhere with you would be wonderful.”

Chapter Eleven

"Beautiful, smart, witty, self-sufficient and wise"

October, for me, meant the annual Seattle Antiquarian Book Fair. The Fair is a two-day show where more than one hundred dealers from all over the country bring their collectible books, prints and ephemera to sell. I had exhibited at every Seattle show since I started my book business in 1987, and it was the highlight of my business year. Not only was it a good opportunity to sell books and meet new and old customers, it was also a great place to buy new material. And this year I wanted Rose to come to the show with me so we could enjoy a weekend in the city together.

The woman I had been with for seventeen years before I married my second wife had a new house with her partner on Queen Anne Hill. We had become the best of friends since we parted, and they graciously offered me their basement apartment during the show to cut down on my expenses.

I was getting more deeply attracted to Rose and I wanted her to see how I made a living. There was also a part of me that worried I was being drawn into a relationship thinking it was "love" when it might just be "lust." But I also knew there was something very different about Rose: Around her, I felt larger than just my physical self. It was hard to put my finger on what was so different about her; she was physically beautiful, smart, witty, self-sufficient and wise without any pretense. She was at ease with herself and with those around her. When I was with her, I felt an intense connection that was at once invigorating and other times enigmatic. But even in her obscure moments, there was a warmth to her evasiveness that drew me to her like a bewitching song. The frankness of her life was like a classic blues progression… elementary yet satisfying in its simplicity.

Rose was frugal but not cheap; if she wanted or needed something she didn't settle for second best. She owned a professional six-burner gas stove that made her a living. She bought Bella the most nutritious kibbles, because she was a working dog who needed to be healthy and fit. She ordered the highest quality baby chicks from a commercial hatchery in the Midwest and had them shipped to the Ranch. She didn't have a huge wardrobe but everything she owned had a distinct style and uniqueness that set her apart from women both older and younger than her. She had a solid sense of how the marketplace worked for what she provided and was happy to buy for a dollar and sell for two. For me, just watching her work and listening to how she thought through her enterprises and actions was informative.

I shared with her how I went about my book business and how important it was for a niche business to retain repeat customers with a constant influx of new inventory. With her market and wholesale egg business, there were things I could help her with to grow new customers in our digital world.

We both had an intense attraction to each other as though we were exchanging the very essences of who we were. And we were not hard on each other. There was no deep-seated drama, no heavy baggage, and no conflicting beliefs or vices to overcome. We talked, we shared, and we had fun together. And I wanted her with me everywhere including the book fair.

"I can't," she said. "Somebody would have to take care of Bella and put the chickens in at night."

"It's just a weekend," I said. "We'll have a place to stay, and we can take in the city together."

"I can't, but I'll come in for a while."

"Saturday then," I said. "Come in on Saturday. We can at least have dinner in the city."

Chapter Twelve

"EVENTS DON'T OCCUR IN A VACUUM."

If I had learned anything from my previous relationships, it was the importance of honesty. I had been criticized at an early age for not talking to my father, and later for not sharing deep feelings with some of the women in my life. I had tried to be open with people close to me, but more times than not they were more interested in their own concerns than they were in mine. Then there were times when my openness was turned against me, and I would completely close down.

With Rose, I never felt a moment of judgment, superiority, or betrayal of confidence. She was a great listener with an inquisitive mind. We talked openly and shared areas of interest without fear of ridicule. She did take great joy in giving me a hard time about my belief in the Seattle Mariners despite their lackluster history. She also liked to chide me about being baptized as a Methodist when I was young even though I hadn't been to church in fifty years. It was her way of having fun with me by focusing on the here and now, not the speculative or ethereal.

I brought her copies of the three books I had written, in part so she could know more about where I had come from. It was one thing to tell someone you are a writer, and another for them to read for themselves what you have created. I told her she was under no obligation to read them, and I would not be offended if she didn't. If she wanted to know some of the events that had shaped my life, she would find a few of them in the books I had written.

One morning while we were having coffee on the back deck, I told her I believed the President Kennedy assassination was more complicated than the lie the world had been sold. I had recently watched an interview with a prominent military advisor during the Kennedy and Johnson administrations, a retired Army colonel and author named Fletcher Prouty, who knew firsthand of a wider network covering up the assassination.

I shared with Rose that on one of my book-buying trips to Dallas, I made a special trip to Dealey Plaza to see for myself where the assassination had occurred. We agreed there is something very powerful about some places, places where important or catastrophic events occurred. Whatever happened in those places, stayed there forever and no matter when you were there you could feel the special energy that place held if you knew of its history.

To my surprise, when I visited Dealey Plaza, it looked exactly as it did in the news reports the day the president was killed, except it felt smaller, more people-sized in person. The plaza was both mysterious and normal at the same time. That place was a reminder that the most momentous acts can occur in the simplest locales. The grassy knoll was once just a patch of grass, and the school book depository was once just an old brick warehouse; but today Dealey Plaza is the monument to the killing field of a president. The splintering effect of that horrific killing still resides in that plaza, on the X-spot in the middle of Elm Street and in the shadow of the depository.

That assassination shattered our generation. It set into motion a new way for the high-placed government officials to conduct the business of America, where the power brokers behind the curtain of normalcy cast the fate of Americans. If a president's actions are not in the power elite's best interests, I told Rose, he can be removed, and if the President of the United States can be executed, then none of us is safe from the madness. Rose and I agreed on the significance of that fateful day in November 1963, and whether we all knew it or not, America was forever changed that day.

"We need to watch the movie 'JFK'," I told Rose. "As I recall, there were a lot of New Orleans locations involved in the plot."

"I haven't seen it since it first came out," she said.

"Then, it would be good to watch it before we go," I said.

I had her dial up YouTube on her Smart TV and search for Fletcher Prouty interviews. Not only was Prouty prominent in the intelligence community but he worked inside the Pentagon and had firsthand involvement in many similar covert actions around the world. Prouty also confirmed he was the basis for the character Mr. X in the movie JFK—the unnamed source of inside information on the killing.

In one particular interview Prouty gave an historical perspective on the mentality that explained the world we live in. As a preface, he went back to the British East India Company which was chartered in 1600 by Queen Elizabeth I to establish trade in the East Indies. The major powers in the age of exploration, including the British East India

Company, realized the Earth and its assets were finite and they set out to assess the world's resources and once located, colonized those regions. Colonization was all about documenting assets and gaining control of the planet's wealth. Corporate shares in those resources were then sold to investment companies. What began as a focus on trade quickly turned to territory acquisition driven by the interests of powerful merchants and aristocrats.

That same mindset is still at play today. Prouty contended the major powers today are still vying for the resources that create wealth, power, and control on a global scale. And those who stand in the way of this pursuit are removed regardless if they are tribesmen, a Third World leader, an activist, a competitor or, in our case, the President of the United States. Prouty knew Kennedy had gotten in the way, as did many other world leaders over the years, of the true power brokers and Kennedy paid the ultimate price.

Rose and I spent a lot of time discussing those events. There is a thread to everything that happens; events and actions don't occur in a vacuum. Events happen for a reason. And I wanted to visit places in New Orleans relevant to events surrounding the assassination.

My life, like so many in my generation, had been affected by the ripple effect of the assassination. I was sixteen when Kennedy was assassinated and with the killing of our President it was like the light had left the day. The unspeakable had happened and all I knew of Kennedy at that time was he was young, good looking and people liked him. It made no sense someone would shoot him, and from that day on my life felt disrupted.

After I graduated from high school, I left home. I had to leave my family to find my own way, and the only thing that felt good was making music. I was in and out of junior college and in 1966 I received my draft notice which led to me enlisting to avoid the infantry. I didn't want to kill anyone or be killed for a war I didn't understand. What had the Vietnamese ever done to Americans? I would spend three and a half years in the army spying on our enemies, but it was during my tour in Panama that I learned our CIA had tracked down and assassinated the Cuban revolutionary Che Guevara in the mountains of Bolivia. I had intercepted a communication from one of Guevara's soldiers that led to my learning of Che's final demise at the hands of our government. After my discharge, I felt lost in a civilian world in which I no longer fit. I got married for stability but resisted domesticity; settling down and having a family was not what I was looking for.

I read books challenging the "lone assassin" theory of Kennedy's death and the more I read the more convinced I was the assassination was more complicated than the immediate explanation we were given.

The Vietnam experience sent me into a depression; not just feeling lost, but empty. There was speculation government officials were involved, and I felt driven into a hole, a solitary place below ground level where I alone tried to find a way out of the confusion surrounding so many of us. After I read Prouty's book on Kennedy and Vietnam, I realized the war was a lie. I learned Kennedy was going to withdraw U.S. forces from Vietnam by the end of 1965 according to his National Security Action Memorandum 263 but with his death in 1963 newly sworn in President Lyndon Johnson reversed that memorandum. From that moment on, the war in Vietnam was given a green light. The result was a grand and bloody deception that sent a generation on the road to heavy consequences. The balance in our lives had been broken into a thousand pieces by that war, and the wounds created in those who returned home never fully healed.

These were not thoughts and beliefs I had openly shared with others in my life, but they flowed easily between Rose and me. In Rose, I found someone who understood the events that shaped our lives and someone open to looking deeper than the surface issues. We were able to be honest with each other without the fear of rejection or ridicule; and for me, the lack of fear of who I was and how I saw the world marked a major step forward in our relationship.

Chapter Thirteen

"I THOUGHT ABOUT YOU THREE TIMES."
- ROSE

The first day and a half of the Seattle book fair had been profitable. I sold some nice books before the show opened and found other items to offer some of my better customers. But by mid-afternoon on Saturday, I was focused on seeing Rose. I kept checking my watch, not knowing exactly what time she would arrive. A few minutes before four, Rose walked into my booth wearing the exhibitor badge I had left for her at the front desk. She was dressed in a long black dress, wearing a silver chain and pendant, her signature beret, and she was a sight for sore eyes.

My soon to-be-ex-wife also had a booth at the fair, and I had concerns she might get spiteful if she saw us together. I would not have put it past her to do something to complicate the divorce, but I was so happy Rose was at the show I didn't care.

The show closed at 6 p.m. on Saturday, and Rose and I immediately left the building and walked the four blocks to the Crow Restaurant. It had become a popular place for exhibiting booksellers during the fair, and the roasted chicken dinner was a popular item on the menu. We got a table for two opposite the front door and I immediately ordered two glasses of wine. I couldn't take my eyes off Rose, and it made me happy to have her in the city with me.

"Has the show been good?" Rose asked.

"It has," I said. "I've made money, and now I'm sitting here with the most beautiful woman in the world."

"This is a nice place," she said. "Bring all your girlfriends here?"

"Only the prettiest," I said. "Are you sure you can't stay the night?"

"I'm sure," she said.

"You come all the way into town and you won't stay with me."

"Not this time."

"It's me," I said. "You don't find me cute and hunky anymore."

"What gave me away?"

"If I were still cute and hunky, you would not go back to the island tonight."

"Maybe there is somebody else."

"I'd have to hurt him," I said. "At least mess with him so he didn't look so cute."

"Wow," she said. "A man who would fight over me. I'm flattered."

"You should be. It's not in my nature to threaten possible suitors."

Booksellers from the show started filing into the restaurant and, while I would acknowledge them with a quick smile or a nod, I couldn't take my attention off Rose for long.

She sat very proper and somewhat reserved, avoiding eye contact with any of my colleagues. I knew we only had a little time together before she had to head back to the island and I didn't want to take away from our limited time together. Our second glass of wine arrived as did our pan-roasted chicken dinners.

"Did you get a chance to look around at the show?" I asked.

"Not so much," she said.

"There are some very special things to see."

"It looked busy."

"Is there anything you're looking for?"

"Not really," she said. "Except maybe old tarot cards or an interesting book on growing marijuana."

"I'll look around and see what's here."

"That would be nice."

"So tell me about Tarot cards?" I said. "They keep popping up with you."

"Personal guidance," she said.

"And you're a believer?"

"We all believe in something," she said.

"But cards?"

"And other things," she said.

"Including what the cards say," I said.

"There are reasons we make the choices we do," she said. "Why would selecting cards be any different?"

"I don't know," I said. "I don't know enough about the Tarot to have an opinion."

"They can help you think about things," she said, "and consider options."

"And you trust your decisions to a deck of cards?"

"I consider all options," she said. "What do you trust in?"

"That's a good question."

"I thought so," she said.

"I guess knowledge. Personal knowledge and gut feelings."

"And that works for you?"

"For the most part. If you live long enough you learn when to trust what life has shown you."

"So what has life shown you?"

"Control of your life can be hard," I said. "If you want to be happy you have to be in control of your life. And control is not easy. It often requires a trade off. So I trust I know what's best for me."

"So is that why you came to see me after the street dance?"

"I came to see you for the same reason you invited me in. I needed to know why I was attracted to you."

"Have you figured out why?" she asked.

"I'm still working on it. And you? Why did you invite me in?"

"You intrigued me," she said. "And you were bold enough to show up."

We finished dinner and our drinks, and Rose asked for the rest of her chicken in a to-go box.

"Did you like the chicken?"

"It was very tasty. I'll take the rest home for Bella. I'll tell her this is from you too," she said.

It was a little after nine. I paid the bill and we slowly made our way to her car two blocks away. If Rose was lucky she could catch the ten o'clock ferry.

"Sure you can't stay?"

"Dinner was very nice, and I'm glad I came in."

"Then stay with me," I said.

"Not tonight. The dinosaurs are waiting."

I leaned back against her car, pulled her to me and kissed her. She pressed her body hard against me and my body responded immediately.

“I want you right here,” I said.

She reached down and grabbed me hard, squeezing me like a lemon. “Don’t,” I said, “unless you mean it.”

“Oh…I mean it…just not tonight.”

“You’re a cruel, cruel woman” I said. ”Why you treat me so mean?”

“You’re still my cute and hunky man, but I’m not going to stay with you tonight.”

“You’re just going to leave me like this?”

“I have no idea what you’re talking about.”

“I’m talking about what you have in your hand.”

“You can easily rub that out.”

“When I have you right here in my arms?”

“You can think of me when you do.”

“Wouldn’t be the same,” I said

“It worked for me,” she said. “I thought about you three times. That’s why I was late.”

”You’re killing me.”

“And I’m going to miss my ferry.” She kissed me and opened her car door. “Sleep tight and think of me if you like.”

She got in her Jeep and started it up. I just stared in at her hoping she would change her mind. Finally she slowly rolled down the window.

“Thank you for a lovely dinner, *El Presidente*.”

“Thanks for coming in and leaving me like this.”

She stepped out of the car, cupped my face in her hands and looked into my eyes. She slowly leaned into me, drawing out the evening's last moment with the light touch to my lips, and then kissed me passionately. She slowly withdrew her lips from mine and, as if moving in slow motion, she gently slid back into her car.

"I'll see you tomorrow night," she said, with a smile and slowly pulled away.

Chapter Fourteen

"TRUTH IS SHE HATED EVERYTHING ABOUT ME."

After the Book Fair, I refocused my attention on my divorce. I had more papers to file and a summons to have served. I had been consulting with a lawyer, who was very helpful in guiding me through the maze of paperwork and timelines, and by early November most of the paperwork had been filed. All that remained was our December 15th court date with the judge.

November 10th was the two-month mark of having met Rose, but it felt like we had known each other forever. Most every Friday night we went to the Rod 'n Gun Club for dinner or music, sometimes just the two of us and other times with friends. Rose was also a member of the Eagles and on Sundays we would have breakfast or brunch with Marian and Mike, and watch the Seahawks. Saturday nights quickly became our steak night at the Ranch.

I wasn't sure how closely Rose paid attention to our timeline together but, because of her being a recent widow, I was aware of time and the necessary healing process. But I was also interested in the state of our relationship.

We were sitting at the kitchen table drinking Happy Coffee when I checked in with Rose.

"Today marks two months," I said.

"Two months?"

"We met September 10th. Two months ago."

"Really?" she said. "Seems like much longer than that."

"How are we doing?"

"Good," she said.

"No problems?"

"No."

"If there are, I'd like to know."

"We're fine," she said.

"You'd say so if they weren't fine."

"You bet," she said. "So how's the new book going?"

For six years I had delivered seminars on book collecting and book selling in over a dozen cities around the country but, with the downturn in the economy and the shrinking number of open shops and regional book fairs, it had become harder to reach potential attendees. I stopped the in-person programs and decided to turn the collecting seminar into a book.

"It's coming along fine," I said. "It's a bit of a pain getting all the illustrations and photos correct, but Denis is making things work."

Denis was a young graphic designer who was designing my collecting book and its cover. He was also married to my unofficial spiritual advisor, Cherub.

"I have a meeting coming up about the cover design," I said. "I'd like you there for your input."

"If you want me there," she said, "I'll be there."

By now Rose and I were spending every free moment together. Most nights we stayed up late talking and I would end up staying over. The Ranch was feeling more and more like home, and my apartment was only where most of my things lived.

I enjoyed Rose's company and, for the first time in over a decade, I felt the woman in my life truly understood me. Part of getting to know someone is just listening and wanting to know who the other person is beyond the surface veneer. There was an atmosphere of openness between us that was established early on with blunt talk about our likes and desires. She was totally at ease with her body and uninhibited when it came to expressing her physical needs and her desire to have me join her in New Orleans. As two adults in our sixties, we didn't have the luxury of time to dance around what was important to us. Time was not our friend, but honesty was. The time we spent together focused on sharing our life stories in small bursts of casual conversation.

A major part of my life now was music; not so much in the amount of time I spent making it, but more how I felt making it. It was a wonderful release and one of the purest forms of expression. I had spent the better part of my life selling or writing about the creative work of others, and now I was actively giving expression to my own creations. And I loved the intimacy performing music live provided. You could write a song on Monday and perform it on Saturday; that sort of immediacy doesn't usually happen in other art forms.

When I got to the Ranch after filing the last of my divorce papers, Rose greeted me with a hug and a big smile on her face.

"You seem in a good mood," I said.

"I am," she said. "I got us tickets to see Jeff Bridges and his band."

"I didn't know he had a band."

"They're at the Edmonds Performance Center. They're called the Abiders. We're ten rows back from the stage."

"Sounds good," I said. "What do they play?"

"A little bit of everything. I've listened to them on line. You'll like it."

I thanked her for thinking of us and getting the tickets. That night while we lay in bed, I told her she missed her calling.

"You should have been a promoter."

"And give up raising dinosaurs? I already promote what I like. I want you to experience whatever can help you."

"My ex never really got me." I said.

"What part?"

"How important music is to me."

"You two never talked about it?"

"I tried repeatedly to explain that playing music was about me. It comes from me. I create it, and it's an expression of who I am. But she only saw it as time not spent on her."

"That could be a problem."

"It was…constantly. Truth is…she hated everything about me."

"I doubt that," she said. "She married you."

"She told me so," I said.

"She said she hated you?"

"To my face. And then she called me a liar and a cheat."

"Those are serious things to say," she said. "Were you a liar and a cheat?"

"Not at all," I said. "And when she refused to apologize, that was the last straw."

That night while we lay in bed, we talked about being honest and how hard it was for people to hide who they really are.

"No one can hide a lie forever," I said. "Eventually the masquerade fails and the truth emerges."

"And your point is?" she said.

"Truth eventually surfaces," I said. "I guess it's my way of saying I have nothing to hide from you."

"I know who you are," she replied.

"Then, tell me!" I said, with a nervous laugh.

"I feel pretty with you," she said, "and appreciated."

"Because you are," I said, "but that has little to do with who I am."

"Yes it does," she said. "More than you think."

Rose leaned over and kissed me, then slowly slipped my hand under her pajama top. I gently ran my hand over her breasts. I felt her flat stomach then ran my fingers back up under her breasts and once again felt the series of ridges beneath them. This time I paused, and Rose immediately responded to my hesitation.

"Yes," she said. "I did."

"Did what?"

"Implants. But I had them removed."

I propped myself up and looked at her intently. "Why would you ever have them in the first place?"

"I thought I needed them," she said.

"What you have are beautiful," I said. "You don't need to do anything to yourself."

"I was young," she said, "and I didn't feel attractive."

"Well don't ever talk about doing anything like that again," I said. "I love the way you look right now. You are perfect. I wouldn't change a thing."

She rolled over and kissed me.

"I'm serious," I said.

"I know you are. That's one of the things I like about you."

Chapter Fifteen

"YOU CAN STILL FIND WHAT YOU'RE LOOKING FOR, IF YOU FOLLOW THE TRAIL BACK. IT COULD BE RIGHT WHERE YOU LEFT IT."
- BOB DYLAN

Ten days before Christmas 2015, my divorce was final and that part of my life legally came to an end. I was beginning my new life and whatever the future held for Rose and me. And that future had nothing to do with things; I left everything but my clothes, my books and my instruments behind when I left my marriage. My future was about something deeper, something I carried inside me. During the three months I had known Rose, my quality of life had gone from dour to joyous and I felt truly alive. I felt like I was learning to be me again.

During my ten-year marriage, I had allowed my life to be dictated by someone else. It was through a series of appeasements, to maintain the peace, that "who I was" slowly devolved into "who someone else wanted me to be." Little by little, I had dissolved into a mere shadow of who I knew I was and what I wanted from life. There was a missing person inside me, and I needed to find him.

When I first consulted a divorce lawyer and explained our dynamics as honestly as I could, he smiled and shook his head.

"This is a classic case of 'what's hers is hers and what's yours is hers," he said. "And that covers everything from finances and property to your interests and dreams."

From that moment on, there was no doubt in my mind what I had allowed to happen and getting a divorce was the right decision.

The Christmas season was a mixed blessing. I was happy to be with Rose and I was looking forward to showing her how much she and the Ranch meant to me. In general, I hated the sense of obligation that came with the holidays, but for the first time in a long while I was looking forward to any opportunity to express my affection for Rose.

Rose didn't display a Christmas tree or the traditional holiday trappings around the house, except for a few items that spoke to her Norwegian background. Rose's given name was Brena Gustafson and she ardently supported the Island's annual Nordic Festival during the holiday season. In many ways Rose exemplified the rural and class-free nature of the few Norwegians I had known. They tended to glorify the simple ways of life and rigorously guarded their personal space. Rose reflected the Norwegian tendency toward an independent and self-sufficient nature that was becoming more apparent the more she shared about her past.

She was not a religious person in the strictest sense of the word, but she did have a spiritual side to her. She wrapped colored lights around a small pine tree on the corner of the front deck as her primary holiday statement. But the house constantly smelled of fresh baked goods and it was a time to think about loved ones. The truth was I had not stopped thinking about Rose since the moment I first met her. I loved her simple lifestyle, her occasionally audacious behavior, and the serious way she undertook her business. That Christmas, Rose was the only gift I needed or desired.

When I first met her in September, I immediately sensed she was someone special-- almost too special to fully absorb at the time. Each day I spent with Rose felt like a day of rebuilding, of replacing the bricks of my being that had been pulled from my foundation. My personal dissolution was not anyone else's doing though. I alone was responsible for the life I had allowed to unfold; and likewise regaining my sense of worth was up to me. Over the ensuing months, Rose made me forget who I had allowed myself to become, and the devitalized life I had been living.

I started taking more days off from the shop, when I wasn't scheduled at the grocery store, to spend more time with Rose. We'd go shopping for cooking and baking supplies off island, have lunch at a little deli she knew served the best Rueben sandwiches and finish the day of errands with a margarita before heading back home.

We made a day trip out of my last visit to the county courthouse and had the quiet town of Coupeville to ourselves. We had lunch at Toby's Tavern and watched playful seals sunning themselves at the end of the town's pier. Rose insisted we take photos of us having fun and clowning around for the camera. She would blow a kiss to the camera (click) then lap her tongue over my cheek just as I snapped the shutter (click). We were like two kids experiencing our first love affair; free spirits oblivious to the world around us, totally focused on ourselves and how happy we were together.

That Christmas I thought hard about a special gift for Rose. I tried to think of something significant that spoke to her and perhaps our relationship. I had told her early on that one of the things I liked about her was that she was "age appropriate." While age alone is not a recipe for a successful relationship, there are connections associated with being with someone who shares your same life experiences. While there were a lot of young women I was attracted to physically, I could not imagine having enough in common with them to carry on an extended conversation. It had been my experience that common ground was the hardest part of a relationship. Most everything else was easier if you were able to share the deepest parts of you.

One night at dinner I asked Rose to make a list of things she would like for Christmas. I had no idea if she needed anything special because she was clearly self-sufficient within her modest lifestyle. Anything she wanted or needed for her business or herself, she would get. I was still getting to know her personally, and I never heard her express a specific desire for anything.

I tore off a sheet of scratch paper and handed it to her. I watched as she took my pen and appeared to give serious thought to what she wanted for Christmas. She started her list and, without looking up from the paper, she made a confession.

"I've checked you out," she said.

"That's good to know. What did you find out?"

"My neighbor Rozie said you're a nice guy. She and Kennedy said everybody likes you."

"I doubt everybody," I said. "My ex and some of her friends would probably disagree."

"Friends rarely know another couple's real story," she said. "It sounds like you were not well-matched."

"It didn't always seem so," I said, "but the longer we were together, the less compatible we became."

I took a drink of my coffee, and then took Rose by the hand.

"Are you having second thoughts about me?"

"I was just asking my friends if this is all too soon."

"To be with someone?"

"I didn't want to seem disrespectful."

"What was the consensus?"

"Rozie said not if I felt okay with it."

"And do you?"

"It feels okay," she said. "But I haven't even buried Bob's ashes yet. They're still sitting right over there." She gestured to the bookcase near the wood stove.

"Do you have plans for Bob?"

"I want to bury him," she said, "but I can't."

"Why not?"

"His estranged daughter won't sign off on what to put on the headstone. I can't even bury him in peace."

When Rose finished her Christmas list, there were ten things on it. Some of them were humorous like a backhoe and a proper drainage system for the chicken area, but the one thing that jumped out at me was a nail gun.

In the three months we had been together Rose and I had talked about the things the house needed. The door and window frames needed trim to finish them off so the house wouldn't look unfinished. I could clearly see us doing a lot of the finish work ourselves with a power saw and a nail gun, so that was the number one item I felt she could use most. I also wanted her to have some personal gifts. She had an old gray bathrobe that was not very warm during winter, so I bought her a heavy white terry cloth robe and a set of black cotton pajamas with little red hearts. I added a pair of black mesh stockings for novelty's sake.

We spent Christmas Eve at Marian's with other "orphan" friends in Rose's tribe who didn't have immediate family nearby. There were seven of us and Marian served her traditional lasagna dinner. The evening was a nice way to celebrate the season with good food, good drink and new friends in a relaxed atmosphere.

I spent Christmas Eve night with Rose and early the next morning before she woke up, I brought her gifts in from my car and put them on the couch. I brewed a cup of Happy Coffee and started a fire to warm the house. While I waited quietly for her to wake up, I turned on the TV and clicked on a video loop of a wood-burning fireplace we had found in a section of novelty videos on YouTube. It gave the room a warm and holiday feeling without going overboard. When I heard Rose stirring in the bedroom, followed by her morning greeting to Bella, I made her a cup of coffee and took it in to her.

"Good morning," I said. "Merry Christmas."

She sat up in bed and I handed her the coffee.

"You're up early," she said.

"A fat man was at the door with some packages."

"Don't you hate that?"

She got out of bed, quickly followed by Bella who was ready for her morning kibbles. By the time I fed Bella and Mr. Kitty, Rose had joined us in the kitchen and we had a proper good morning embrace. Rose was even cuter in her half-asleep-in-a-fog state. I pulled her close to me, feeling very lucky to have this beautiful woman in my life. She made that Christmas more special, even without all the holiday decorations and music. I was happier that Christmas than I had been in a long, long time. There was no pretense, no obligation to be happy because we were happy. Rose was a joy to be with regardless of the day, but that day I was prepared to show her how committed I was to her and our future. For me the nail gun, while not a traditional Christmas gift for a woman by any means, spoke to my commitment to help her finish the house and make it even homier.

When she opened the package and saw what it was, she was clearly pleased.

"It's completely self-contained," I said, "with its own compressor and a variety of nail options."

"It's perfect," she said.

"We can do the finish work here ourselves."

"Yes we can," she said, "but not before the Ranch is settled. I don't want to do anything to improve the property, until it has been appraised and is in my name."

"We have the tools now," I said, "and once the property is yours we can get started."

"Thank you so much." She came over and gave me a passionate kiss. Bella jumped up between us and nuzzled her nose between our faces.

"Bella approves," she said.

She unwrapped her new bathrobe and immediately put it on. My gifts included a new pair of slippers which I needed badly and a nice Zippo lighter. I had told her I honestly didn't need or want anything more in my life, but I was happy with what she gave me.

"Just having you is gift enough," I said.

Chapter Sixteen

"THE POWER OF PLACE."

With Christmas behind us and my divorce final, I was looking forward to the New Year and a new beginning. Rose and I spent New Year's Eve having dinner at the Rod 'n Gun Club with Marian and Mike, then the four of us welcomed in the New Year at the pub across from my apartment. Everybody was in good spirits and we talked about our upcoming trip to New Orleans. For Mike and me, it was our maiden voyage to the Big Easy; for Rose and Marian it was a return visit and they discussed clubs to visit and an after-party they said would be the highlight of parade night.

Rose showed us a picture of the building where our room was in the French Quarter. We were in a three-story Old World apartment building with iron railings wrapped around the balconies overlooking Royal Street. Even though I had never been to

New Orleans, it was a place that I knew through my reading and my writing influences. As an apprentice writer, my earliest influence was Sherwood Anderson and his story-cycle Winesburg, Ohio. Anderson was originally from Ohio, but he spent time in New Orleans where he befriended and mentored the young William Faulkner. The playwright Tennessee Williams also spent a lot of time in the French Quarter, using it as the backdrop for some of his best work including *A Street Car Named Desire.* I was greatly influenced by these writers, and I was looking forward to absorbing the atmosphere that inspired their writing.

I had long believed in the power of place. In my travels, I had felt the energy of Dealey Plaza, the spirit of Thoreau's Walden Pond, the pirate battles fought in Portobello, Panama, and even the musical energy of L.A.'s Sunset Strip. The spirit of a place can be very powerful, just as a person's life force, if you are open to what has transpired there. Powerful events can have a lasting impact on the place where they occur; place can hold the essence of those events and retain it for those who come to it later. I knew we were going to a city with a rich literary and music history, and I was prepared to absorb as much of it as possible. I made notes on the Kennedy-related places I wanted to see and the names of bookstores to visit as well as some literary landmarks.

Rose had already received the keys to our room, and she had prepared a package to mail to the address. In the package would be enough herbal amusement for five days.

Chapter Seventeen

"The Rose of Bourbon Street."

We flew out of Seattle on Thursday January 29, 2015 with a stop in Los Angeles before flying on to New Orleans, arriving early that evening. We took a cab into the Quarter and the driver, a jovial African American woman named Tootie, dropped us off at our address on Royal Street between St. Anne and Dumaine Streets. At street level, our building was nondescript on the outside. We made our way through a locked iron street gate that led to a long hallway, then to another secured interior gate. Once inside the building proper, we climbed the three circular flights of stairs and unlocked a third door to an outside patio area and finally the door to our room.

The room was tiny with a small closet to the right of the front door. A small refrigerator and a microwave sat on a table with glasses and cups for two. The large bed cut the room in half with a toilet and separate shower on the other side. A small TV was mounted high up on the wall opposite the head of the bed. It was basically an efficiency room with an open air patio right outside that was somewhat secluded from the floor of rooms above us. A round metal table with two cushioned chairs was the centerpiece of the patio. Opposite the sitting area was a lattice wall heavily draped with years of colorful beads from past Mardi Gras celebrations. The patio was quiet except for the occasional sound of music from out on the street.

"Is this going to be okay?" Rose asked.

"It'll be perfect," I said.

"Are you sure? We could see about something else…Something nicer."

"I'm positive."

"I had booked it just for me," she said. "I wasn't looking for anything extravagant when I booked it."

"It's got everything we need," I said.

The room couldn't have been more than 150 square feet in size, but it was all we needed, and I liked the outside patio. The room reminded me of a Paris garret I had once stayed in, except this space had the bathroom in the room. I could see a writer living there except there wasn't room for a writing table. The writer would have to write on the patio or, in inclement weather, in a café. But for our purposes the room was all we needed. Besides I was more focused on the company and the city than I was on the niceties of a room.

The package Rose had mailed was waiting for us on the bed, and she immediately removed the contents. We quickly assessed we would need a few supplies like coffee and Irish Crème for Happy Coffee in the morning, and some late night snacks. A small grocery store called Rouses sat on the corner across the street from us that would certainly satisfy our basic needs.

Rose put a call into Marian, who had arrived the day before us, to let her know we were in town and make plans to meet up. Marian and Mike had rented a large shotgun apartment out in the Marigny district, about fifteen minutes by cab from the Quarter. After we unpacked, we went out onto the patio and had a smoke before going out into the night life.

Royal Street was quiet, except for the distant sound of a lone saxophone echoing off the brick street. We walked up a block to Bourbon Street where the air was abuzz with competing sounds of music. The street and sidewalks were full of people strolling past street performers and club barkers. After spending most of the day traveling it was good to walk in the fresh air and, for me, to absorb the new environs.

The architecture was the first thing I noticed. The two and three-story buildings had a strong European feel to them, fronting narrow streets, some of them bricked, with balconies draped in ivy over ornate, wrought-iron railings. Small, dimly-lit shops of all descriptions were bordered by bars with bright lights and neon. People were everywhere, walking in the middle of the street, on the sidewalks, roaming from bar to bar, catching blasts of music echoing off the nearby buildings.

It was the beginning of Mardi Gras and also Super Bowl weekend, and our Seattle Seahawks were in the Big Game. Our timing couldn't have been better to be in a city where the ribald, the festive and the sublime all exist in the same place at the same time. We walked down one side of Bourbon Street and up the other, then went into a bar, got two gin and tonics in plastic cups, and continued walking in the cool night air. We had not eaten in a while, but neither of us felt like trying to find a proper restaurant at that hour.

We strolled up Bourbon Street pausing periodically to listen to the live music spilling out into the street. A few blocks further Rose pointed to a street vendor.

"Lucky Dogs!" she said. "The best street food in town."

We ordered two chili dogs that were big, tasty and more than filling. Dinner for two under ten dollars and we were feeling good. We finished our street dinner and continued our stroll in the crisp night air. We paused periodically to take in more music and the various street performers ranging from jugglers and fire-eaters to a human Transformer. What started out as a 3-foot by 3-foot bright yellow cardboard car in the middle of the street suddenly morphed into a young man in the form of a human robot then slowly folded back into the small yellow cardboard car that actually rolled on wheels.

At one point we strolled far enough from the music clubs and the other visitors that we suddenly found ourselves alone. Rose stood in the middle of Bourbon Street, with her long brown hair draped around her face. Behind her, the damp street glistened under the rainbow of red, yellow and blue neon lights glowing from the clubs. The scene looked as if time had stopped and Rose owned the town.

"Hold it right there," I said. "Don't move."

I took out my phone, launched the camera and centered Rose on the screen. She was alone in the street with no traffic, looking over her left shoulder at me. She was the most beautiful sight I could imagine.

Rose made everything around her stand still and I snapped the picture. I had forgotten to make sure the flash was on but her image was there. Later, she would tell me it was her favorite photograph, and I could see why. She looked stunning and youthful. I titled the picture "Rose on Bourbon Street." A year and a half later, I would write a song for Rose entitled "The Rose of Bourbon Street" inspired by that photo.

We made our way back to Royal Street and went into Rouses grocery. We bought a bottle of Bailey's and a jar of Turkish coffee. I remembered reading somewhere Tennessee Williams frequented Rouses when he lived in the Quarter, and for just a moment it made the shopping experience that much more special.

We went back to our room and despite the full day of travel, we still found enough energy to christen our first night in the Big Easy with a wonderful evening of intimacy. It made for the perfect start for what I could feel was going to be an important trip.

Chapter Eighteen

"A MAN WHO CAN MAKE MUSIC
WILL NEVER BE ALONE."

On our first morning in New Orleans we got up late, and I made us two cups of Happy Coffee and we took them out onto the patio. The morning air was chilly but the hot coffee and the Irish Crème took the nip out of the air and we discussed our plans for the day.

New Orleans was Rose's town and I left our itinerary up to her. I was her guest or better yet I was her subject. As it turned out, she had a clear idea of what this trip would be for me and for us. The only things on my personal agenda were to visit several bookstores and the JFK locations, and connect with my literary and blues interests.

Because of my interest in blues music, musicians and their folklore, I was aware that there are certain icons constantly referred to like spirits, tricksters, and magic potions. One of the most prominent is the

Mojo Bag. Muddy Waters and many other old bluesmen refer to it along with something called a John the Congeroo root. Rose and I had several conversations early on about blues lore and the magical references the African American players incorporated in their music. They were clearly powerful forces in their lives and I was intrigued by that aspect of the Blues.

Rose said there are some places you have to experience in New Orleans and getting beignets at the Café du Monde on Decatur Street was one of those places. We went over to St. Anne Street and walked the two blocks toward the river and entered the open-air cafe. We sat at a small outside table for two and ordered a plate of beignets and two coffees. The café, established in 1862, had a definite French feel to it with its wrought iron artifice and small round tables in an open structure. The sun broke out sporadically, and it felt good to just relax in the sun, sipping coffee with someone you loved to be with. I can't say I took to the French version of the donut, but I was glad to have had them once. And the fact Rose felt I should experience them was good enough for me. We finished our beignets then walked down to the river.

The Mississippi River is such an iconic part of American history. Between Mark Twain's legacy and the delta blues region up north, the river was an important part of our literary and music folklore. Looking out at the broad swath of water cutting through the city, I could see how its power and dominance shaped much of the South. It provided life, and I could feel its immense energy surging passed us. I could envision large paddle-wheelers plying northward and hear the sound of laborers unloading bales of cotton and products heading up north. I took a picture of Rose with the river and Algiers Point in the background to remember my first look at what the Spanish called, the River of the Holy Spirit.

I looked out over the broad waterway and focused on the slow moving current to the point where I no longer felt like I was standing on the levee. The longer I stared out at the river flow, the more muscular it felt; no splashing about or churning rapids, just a slow, plodding force of nature with its own history of secrets and wonder. A presence hovered over the river, a spirit with a life of its own dancing around with enough force to make me look around once then back over my shoulder.

Rose stepped behind me and wrapped her arms around my chest. "Don't you just feel it?" she said

"I do," I said. "I do."

We continued our walk along the levee, and I thought about all the different cultures that melded here: The French, the Spanish, African slaves, and Caribs all intermingled into a huge pot of cultural gumbo. Together their different customs and art forms brought us music not found anywhere else. Jazz infused with blues progressions from the delta region and African rhythms from the Caribbean islands were all mixed together.

We strolled back to Decatur Street, just as many of the small, brightly painted shops were opening for the day.

"I love the architecture," I told her as we walked, "and the colors. Everything feels so original."

"It feels like home," Rose said.

"Home like the Ranch?"

"Home…like it's me," she said.

"I can see you here," I said.

"I keep coming back. You know how some places feel like you."

"I do," I said. I could feel the pull of the river as it slowly rolled by us on its way to the gulf. Even though it cut through the city like a gash in the land, the Mississippi also felt like a connective tissue that married the physical landscape to the unbridled spirit of the people who lived along it.

A couple blocks from the Café du Monde, we came upon a shop that brought Rose to a halt.

"Here it is," she said.

I looked up at the shop sign hanging over the sidewalk that read: "Hex—Old World Witchery." There was a middle-aged woman sitting at a small table in the window reading, with a red curtain separating her from the interior of the shop.

"What is it?" I said.

"You said you wanted a mojo bag," she said.

"I did?"

"The night you talked about the magic in blues music. We talked about tarot cards and you mentioned a powerful root."

"I didn't expect you to remember that," I said.

"Well, this is where you'll find it," she said.

"Is this going to be weird?"

"Of course," she said, "but they should have what you're looking for."

"I'm not looking for a séance or palm reading," I said.

"Come on," she said, and opened the shop door.

The shop was small inside with a dark wood interior, and it smelled of pungent oils and dried flowers. The young man behind the counter was backed by a wall of small wood drawers much like the old card catalog files once found in libraries. A nice selection of beautiful gem stones and crystals filled the glass counter display case.

Rose led me to a self-serve area with containers of different minerals, oils, and herbs. A chart on the wall explained the virtues of each item and below the chart was a selection of small, colored bags.

"First…choose a bag," Rose said. "Then select the things you want in it. I'll be over here looking at tarot cards."

From the chart on the wall I selected a gold bag because it represented wealth and protection. I was not a practitioner of the magic arts but given my interest in blues music I did come across a lot of references to witchery; and belief, whatever form it takes, can be a powerful agent in life. The belief in a higher power, the belief in things happening for a reason, or the belief in oneself, can often be the difference between success and failure, joy and despair.

I was intrigued by the old bluesmen's belief in such magic and how it affected and informed their lives and the music they made. There were so many magic references in their music that it was hard to ignore the power it held for them. There were references to black cat bones that could grant someone invisibility, goofer dust for casting a spell, and ju-ju charms. So I was both curious and willing to investigate and see what a mojo bag might do in my life.

I looked over the various options and considered what each one was purported to address.

I first chose a piece of *fluorite* because the description said it would clear away negativity and help restore emotional balance. After my divorce, I was in dire need of clarity and balance. *Fluorite* was also said to help manifest ideas and bring plans to fruition. It was also supposed to help with brain chatter and give you access to deeper truths. That all sounded like a good place to start.

I read over some of the other issues on the chart and was drawn to *bloodstone.* Since I had been treated for a form of leukemia two years earlier, I was sensitive to anything dealing with blood concerns. *Bloodstone* was supposed to be conducive to treating blood disorders, so that was an obvious choice. It was also supposed to help those who have been abandoned by others and help the possessor know that loneliness and isolation are mere illusions. I thought of Rose and how she had mentioned in passing one night her mother had left her at a young age. I didn't press the issue at the time, but I felt having that stone wouldn't hurt either of us.

A piece of *pyrite* caught my attention, and the description said it would overcome feelings of inadequacy and help you live your life to its fullest potential. I quickly added it to my bag.

Citrine was believed to carry the power of the sun and was life-giving. The description said it would awaken creativity and imagination. I hadn't written any new music in a while and, except for the book-collecting book, nothing of book-length in years. It was also supposed to help transfer dreams and wishes into tangible results. At the time, my strongest wish was that my life with Rose continue to grow and intensify. Supposedly, carrying *citrine* attracts love and happiness and guards against those who would break your heart. That piece of quartz went straight into my bag.

Rose came up next to me and put her arm around me while I searched the remaining stones and herbs for the one item I had heard so much about.

"They don't have it," I said to her in a whisper.

"What don't they have?" she whispered back.

"The root. The blues root."

"Why are we whispering?" she said.

"I don't know. Kind of feels like church."

"You Methodists. Did you look at everything?"

"It's not here."

"Maybe it has another name," she said.

"Maybe it's a myth."

"You should ask," she said.

I went to the counter and asked the young man for the congeroo root.

"What's it called?" he said

"John the congeroo," I said. "It's mentioned in a lot of blues music."

"I'm not familiar...." he started to say, when the woman who had been sitting in the front window stepped behind the counter.

"You're looking for something specific?" she said.

"John the congeroo. It's something mentioned in a lot of blues songs."

"Yes of course," she said. She bent down and pulled a small jar out from a shelf below and set it on the counter. "It's called John the Conqueror. It's a root related to the sweet potato." She removed a small piece of dark dried root that didn't look at all special and put it on the counter.

"So that's it," I said. "For some reason I expected something... well... special looking."

"It is said to bring good luck," the woman said, "and enhance sexual powers."

"Well alright," Rose said, "lucky us."

"Any idea who this John is?" I asked.

"Supposedly, it was named after a slave who refused to be subservient. He acquired the characteristics of a mythical trickster, and just mentioning his name was a powerful spell of magic protection."

"I've got to have it," I said.

"Jason will take care of you," the woman said. She smiled and returned to her window table and drew the bright red curtain closed behind her.

"Did you find any cards?"

"I did," Rose said.

I paid for our treasures, and Rose decided we should just walk and take in the neighborhoods on foot. The sun was out and we were both feeling good about what we had acquired.

We walked back to Royal Street and headed for the Marigny District. Many of the two and three-story apartment buildings were draped with colorful displays of costumed mannequins, giant masks, balconies dressed with purple, gold, and green banners, porch pillars wrapped in colorful beads, and doors covered with *fleur-de-lis* emblems.

Once we got out of the bustle of the French Quarter, the energy level on the street grew quieter and our gait more leisurely. I held Rose's hand as we walked and it was like we were in a slow dance, floating on a carousel of fresh sights and new shapes. The landscape swirled around us, and if there had been a soundtrack it would have been a Cajun waltz played through a lone accordion.

Some of the small houses along the narrow street were guarded by iron gates, and shotgun houses were built right up to the sidewalks, dressed in pink and blue paint with bright red doors. Occasionally a larger house was set back from the street with a walkway draped in palm fronds leading away from the damp street to a cool patio.

I was quickly transported to a much older time, and I could hear the laughter of children and the occasional bark of a dog. The buildings were low and close to the ground, and the black and white faces we passed on the street were animated with an ease not usually seen in big cities.

I stopped at the corner of Chartres and Decatur Streets and just looked around.

"I love this place," I said.

"Me too."

"Listen how quiet it is."

We stood there a minute and listened. I turned to Rose and smiled.

"I love you madly," I said and kissed her.

"No you don't," she said.

"But I do."

"You're just happy because you had me last night."

"I'm serious," I said. "I can't remember the last time I felt this good."

"Let's keep walking," she said. "There's a nice little place up ahead where we can get a drink."

We continued up Decatur where it jogged onto Frenchman Street. Two blocks later we came to a bistro on the corner of Royal Street.

The Marigny Brasserie sat right on the corner of Royal and Frenchman Streets and had just opened for lunch. The sun was still out so we took one of the tables outside that faced the sun. We ordered two screwdrivers and agreed to split a roasted turkey sandwich with a side of garlic mashed potatoes.

The brasserie was in the middle of a neighborhood with none of the tall office buildings of down town or the string of all night bars in the Quarter. It was completely removed from the tourist area and it felt like we were home on the island on a weekday without tourists.

The sun felt good on my face and I looked over at Rose in her bandana and her large sunglasses and I felt extremely lucky.

"I didn't mean to put you off back at the corner," I said.

"Don't worry about it," she said.

"I want you to know how I feel," I said.

The waiter brought our drinks, and I lit a cigarette.

"Cheers," Rose said.

"I just don't want to make the same mistakes I've made before."

"You haven't made any mistakes."

"I've been told I haven't been the best communicator."

"You communicate just fine," she said.

"I'm talking about deep things. Things that really matter. When I'm with you, I want you to know how I feel. I don't want honest things left unsaid."

"I feel the same way."

"I just want to be open and clear with you. You are very special to me, and I want you to know that."

Our food arrived and we each took half of the sandwich. We were the only people at the café, and there were not many people out on the street yet.

"Hear that?" Rose said.

I stopped chewing and listened.

"It's a guitar," I said.

We both looked around the street and listened harder. There were no visible clubs nearby, but kitty-corner from us was Washington Square Park. There was an older African American man sitting on a patch of grass next to the sidewalk. He was leaning against a concrete wall, plucking a guitar ever so lightly.

"I love that about this town," Rose said.

"I do too. It's everywhere."

"You would fit right in here," she said.

"There's a lot of jazz players here."

"There's a lot of everything here, including blues."

"Don't get me wrong," I said. "I love all the horns, but I just don't play that music."

"There's a place here for everything if it's good. You would do fine."

"That's something else I love about you."

"What?"

"Your optimism."

"You are very talented, and I know you would fit right in here."

"You're pretty damn sure of yourself, young lady."

"I like to think I see things in people."

"Like what?" I asked.

"Possibilities."

"What should I see in you?"

"I think you've already seen it," she said.

We finished our lunch and drinks, and I paid the bill. Rose guided me by the arm across the street to where the man with the guitar was playing. We approached the older black man with his well-worn acoustic guitar and his felt hat on the ground in front of him. Rose greeted the man and we listened to him play a simple rendition of "The Sky is Crying," a blues standard written by Elmore James in the 50's. I sang a verse with him and received the hint of a smile for my efforts. We listened to him finish the song, then Rose put a five-dollar bill in his hat. I reached in my pocket, pulled out some singles and added them to his hat.

"Thank you for playing for us," Rose said.

"My pleasure, *Cher*."

Seeing the old man playing reminded me of my time in Spain and the old man I saw in Valencia's main plaza every day. The play I wrote about that Spaniard made me wonder what this man's story was. Where did he come from? What had happened to him in his life? What darkness brought him to this patch of grass with his guitar? Who loved him, or did anyone care at that moment? I had been that black man, been where his heart was at that moment, and knew him well. Seeing him alone plucking his guitar made me feel like the luckiest man in the world to have Rose in my life.

I have a deep respect for solo performers who put themselves out in the world with whatever talent they have and share it. I liked that Rose had that same appreciation. It wasn't always about how much talent someone had; it was more about sharing whatever you felt was your gift, no matter how large or small your talent. People recognize when your offering is real and honest. Clearly we both had an appreciation for solo street players which to my mind is the hardest act and takes a lot of confidence.

We thanked the old bluesman again and left him to play his songs to others walking along Frenchman Street.

We slowly walked back towards the Brasserie. "So what do you think that man's story is?" I asked.

"Bad luck and hard times," Rose said.

"How bad?"

"Could be real bad," she said. "Maybe he's trying to make something good out of the bad."

"But by the grace of God…." I said.

"I don't think a God has anything to do with it," she said.

"He could be any of us."

"I'll remember him doing something good for us," she said. "Let's take Frenchman back. Out here is where a lot of the real music happens."

Halfway down the block a small crowd of people stood outside an old narrow two-story building with steel beams out front that were either holding the structure up or served as scaffolding for remodeling work, perhaps both. A sign in the doorway read: Live music, no cover. We pressed our way past people gathered around the doorway and went inside.

The Spotted Cat Music Club was a small bar with a little stage off to the left of the front door; on the wall adjacent the stage was a very large painting of a hep cat, playing a saxophone with the name of the club painted around it. Like a lot of the older buildings here, the interior was longer than it was wide. The bar ran down the left side of the building and sat maybe twenty people. A dozen more stools were against the wall opposite the bar. Just inside the door the small stage faced an even smaller area for dancing.

The bar was pretty full for a Friday afternoon and it was far enough away from the Quarter that the chances were good most of the people were either locals or adventurous visitors. We took two available seats at the bar and ordered two screwdrivers. A man we had passed outside stepped up onto the stage and picked up his guitar. He started playing an old blues lick and singing a song I was not familiar with.

"So what do you think?" Rose said.

"I love it."

"Thought you might." She looked around like she was sizing up the place or making sure nothing was going to fall down on us.

"So you knew of this place?" I said.

"I've been here before. I like its funky atmosphere."

"It certainly has that," I said, "in a good way."

"That could be you up on the stage," she said.

People in the bar were actually listening to the singer and for a place as bustling as it was, I found that unusual. The singer finished his song and slipped a harmonica into his neck rack and blew an intro into a song he said he wrote for an old lover.

We ordered a second drink and listened to the player finish his second set. The place had totally filled up, with standing room only, and the crowd was attentive. I considered myself a student of many things including performers and their performances. What I enjoy most about seeing performers live is how they play an audience. Do they just play songs? How do they engage the audience? Do they tell stories? Or do they say nothing at all. I wanted to learn as much as I could from other players regardless of the music or the venue.

"This guy has been around," I said to Rose.

"He's pretty good."

"He hasn't lost the crowd, and that's everything when you're solo."

"It's the stories," she said. "You want to know what came from the story so you listen."

The singer finished the last of his brief set, thanked the crowd and reminded everyone there was a tip jar up front.

We finished our drinks and squeezed our way through the crowd standing between us and the front door. Outside, there were people drinking from plastic cups and talking. I saw the guitar player come out with his guitar and immediately light up a smoke and begin talking to people outside. I waited for a break in their conversation then approached him with a five dollar bill.

"I didn't make it to your tip jar," I said.

"Thanks, man."

"I like what you did in there."

"My pleasure."

"I take it you play here a lot."

"Have to," he said. "Like a shark…you keep moving from gig to gig. I'm on my way to another bar to play another set."

"Enough to make a living?"

"It's what I do, man."

"Strictly solo?"

"Hell no. I'm in three different bands. It takes a lot of playing to stay alive. But I love it."

"Well…we enjoyed it a lot," Rose said.

"Thank you, ma'am," he said, reaching for his guitar. "If you'll excuse me, I gotta move."

We continued our walking tour along Frenchman and near Decatur Street Rose led me into The Louisiana Music Factory. I was really interested in getting some music of the region and began looking through the various sections devoted to Cajun and Zydeco music. All of the names were new to me and it was daunting trying to choose a representative CD. While I flipped through the hundreds of artists, Rose talked to a woman in a small cubicle near the front door. A large banner on the back wall of the cubicle read: WWOZ Swamp Shop. I gave up trying to select a CD and joined Rose.

"And we'd like four tickets to the after party," Rose said.

"Sorry," the woman said. "They sold out two days ago."

"Oh damn."

"What did we miss?" I asked.

"The after party. It's the high light of the Krewe du Vieux parade. Big party with lots of good music. The Nevell Brothers headlined the last one I attended."

"And the tickets are gone?"

"Sorry," the woman said.

"I told Marian we should have bought them a week ago."

"We're here from Washington State," I said. "My first Mardi Gras."

"We're so happy to have you," the woman said. "What I can do for you is make you official members of our Krewe du Oz."

"What do we have to do?"

"There's usually a membership fee," she said, "but, since you came all this way, there won't be any charge."

"Sweet."

She gave us each a beautiful gold and black medallion the size of a silver dollar and as heavy as a roll of dimes. It was ornately inscribed with: "Krewe of Wild Ozilians" on one side and on the reverse "WWOZ — Guardians of the Groove."

"You are now officially members of the station's Krewe."

"Will it get us a free drink anywhere?" I asked.

"I don't think so," she said, "but you're surely one of us.

We left the record store with our beautiful Krewe du Oz medallions and the bad news we were not going to the after party. Rose put a call in to Marian to give her the news and make alternate plans.

The sun was still out and though it was a bit brisk, the sun's warmth felt good on my face. I did not bring any sunglasses with me so Rose suggested we stroll through the French Market and see what we could find. We started back toward the Quarter and a short ways down the street Rose pointed to a building across the street.

"We'll be going there tonight," she said.

"What's there?" I asked, squinting to see the name of the business.

"The Blue Nile Club," she said. "Marian said Kermit Ruffin is playing tonight. You'll like him. My friends Joanie and Jimmy are going to meet us there."

Rose had met Joanie and Jimmy years earlier on a visit to Mississippi. They lived in Mobile, Alabama just a few hours from New Orleans and made the drive at least once a month for the music. They had just rented an apartment in the Marigny District with another couple and wanted to show it to Rose.

We continued down Frenchman and followed Decatur back to the Quarter. The French Market was bustling with people as we strolled through it looking for sunglasses. The market was an interesting mix of handcrafted items and imported goods from everywhere. Vendors offered leather bags, jewelry, glassware, and clothing spread out over several blocks of the covered, open-air structure. We walked the length of it until I saw a booth with a variety of hats. I looked through all the styles the Asian seller had and purchased a black felt outback style that would shade my eyes. A few stalls down I found a pair of sunglasses with skinny rims that glowed in the dark.

It had been a long day of walking and we were getting tired and hungry. We crossed Decatur Street and went to the Central Grocery which Rose said was known for its muffulettas. This classic Italian sandwich is filled with Italian meats, two kinds of cheese, and a special marinated pickled olive spread on a large, round sesame loaf. The Central Grocery had made the sandwich famous, and Rose insisted we couldn't come to New Orleans and not have one. So we ordered two of the huge sandwiches to go.

At nine o'clock that night, we took a cab to the Blue Nile and met Marian and Mike outside the club. The blue neon lights lit up the front windows of the club like a warm fog. The night air was cool so we went right in and grabbed a stand-up table in clear view of the stage. The club was not that crowded when we got there, but by the time we finished our first round of drinks the house was near full with more people streaming in. Joanie and Jimmy arrived shortly before the music started and Rose made our introductions.

Joanie was a singer in her sixties with blonde hair, and a deep, raspy voice from years of smoking and whiskey shots. Jimmy was lean, clean-cut and still selling insurance when not making a little music. With our common interest in music and Rose, the conversation flowed easily. That night I learned Rose had been married to a man who worked in Alaska and had met Joanie in the 90s at a club she sang at for almost five years.

By the time Kermit took the stage with his band, the club was standing room only. Kermit is a great performer: He has an infectious voice and blows a mean New Orleans trumpet. Rose said he was featured in an HBO series called *Treme* set in New Orleans post-Katrina along with other great local musicians.

The band was hot that night and the club was hopping from their opening number. It was good to hear live rhythm and blues with a big horn section. Rose and I stayed until eleven before we called it a long, well-travelled day. Marian and Mike headed back to their apartment and Rose and I arranged to meet Joanie and Jimmy the following night for a late drink after the Krewe du Vieux parade and see their new apartment.

Rose and I had spent the whole day taking in as much as we could of life outside the Quarter. She clearly had a plan in mind and since I was new to the city, I was open to whatever she felt was important. Most of what we took in were the subtle aspects of the city: the places where the locals lived, where they played and the music they listened to. It had been a great first day in New Orleans, and I felt invigorated by all the music we heard.

Chapter Nineteen

"Does not a real culture...consist, first of all, in the acceptance of life, life of the flesh, mind and spirit?"
- Sherwood Anderson

Saturday January 31st was the night of the Krewe du Vieux parade. We had arranged to meet Marian and Mike at their rental in the Marigny District before the parade, which began at dusk. But before we took in the Mardi Gras festivities that night, Rose had agreed to help me find the bookstores I wanted to visit. This for me was the business part of the trip, and Rose was happy to help me find the stores.

New Orleans has a rich literary history and I could already feel the influence the city and, especially the French Quarter, must have had on the playwright Tennessee Williams. He had called New Orleans "The last frontier of Bohemia," and the designation still applied. As Rose and I wandered the side streets of the Quarter, I could feel the compression the narrow streets had on me.

The cross-section of people we passed on the streets emanated a sense that no behavior seemed inappropriate. Even the drunks held promise they may have insights that might change my life. Lost souls hovered from the above-ground tombs and gothic vendors hawked the wares of spirits. Private lives hinted there were stories to tell, hidden behind parlor windows, louvered shutters and walled-in courtyards. No wide-open vistas drew me away from where I was at the moment and whatever was unfolding around me. The Quarter had its extremes and eccentrics with everything draped in a bougainvillea mist, and I could feel spirits radiating from the narrow streets.

I thought about the old bluesman we heard at Washington Square Park the day before and how alone he looked. I had known that feeling all too well but I didn't feel it now. Even when I was married I felt more alone than ever. Thinking about that old bluesman made me sad for him, and at the same time I felt like the luckiest man in the world to have Rose in my life.

I was walking the same streets that some of the writers I most respected had roamed, and I was with someone who didn't make me feel alone. I felt the bohemian spirit Williams spoke of. Everything felt creative: the free-form colors of the houses, the street musicians, the vibrant clubs, the artworks strung over rope lines in the alleyways, even the street acrobats we had watched at Waterfront Park.

Rose helped me find the bookstores I was looking for and one by one I perused their modest offerings. I bought a few books at Crescent City Books, and at the Heritage New Orleans Collection I purchased a new book on blues guitarist Lonnie Johnson.

On our way back to Royal Street we were greeted by a wedding procession that suddenly appeared out of nowhere. These public street theatrics, Rose told me, were commonplace in New Orleans, both the religious and the secular. There were public processions for mourners of the dead, marches for the newly-wed, and organized parades for the socially engaged. The one common thread to these various public manifestations was a sense of moving forward, people joined together moving in the same direction. They are a tradition in New Orleans where the locals openly celebrate life, death, and the spirit of being alive. In New Orleans, self-expression was more than a right; it was an art form, whether it was conveyed in a costume, a song, or a marriage parade.

The bride in this procession wore a long pink dress and a crown of beautiful pink feathers. The groom was dressed in a white suit with a bright red cummerbund and a white top hat. A small brass band led the procession, followed by the bride and groom and their family and friends. While the family and friends threw candy to passersby, a young man pulled a string of three little red wagons filled with ice and cans of Pabst Blue Ribbon which he threw to people on the sidewalk. We walked along with the wedding party, taking part as witnesses to the couple's joy, until they turned off onto Bourbon Street and we parted company.

In March of 1925, the novelist William Faulkner came to New Orleans to visit the writer Sherwood Anderson. Faulkner moved into the ground floor apartment at 624 Orleans Avenue, a quaint little street now called Pirate's Alley in the heart of the Quarter. The Alley is adjacent to St Anthony's Garden at the rear of the St. Louis Cathedral, just a block from our room. That Saturday there were several artists displaying their art works in the Alley. Halfway down the Alley was a bookshop where Faulkner once lived, and where he began work on his first published novel, "Soldier's Pay."

Faulkner House Books was small and well-appointed with dark walnut bookshelves and a round display table in what would have been Faulkner's small living room. I had told Rose what I knew of the history of the space before we got there so she might have an enhanced appreciation of the creative mojo the space might hold.

"Can you feel the writer in this space?" I whispered.

"It's a place with spirit," she said. "I can see a writer here."

Rose had an artist's soul in the way she responded to the creative efforts of others, regardless if they were a lone street musician or a known performer like Kermit Ruffin. Rose was as open to new experiences as I was open to her, and I trusted her judgment and perspective. We both had similar yet different perspectives of the creative world that fed us both. She was a facilitator, quietly molding the experience of those closest to her; in that respect she reminded me of the woman I had been with for seventeen years in Seattle. She too was a shaper. Without her, I doubt my previous books would have been finished, let alone published. As I absorbed the energy of Faulkner's one time apartment, knowing how Sherwood Anderson had encouraged him to write, I realized Rose too had come into my life for a reason.

I bought one book at Faulkner House then decided Rose had earned a drink for indulging my book-scouting desire. We walked a few doors down the alley to a small bar called Pirate's Alley Café with outdoor seating in the sun and ordered drinks.

"So what did you buy?" Rose asked.

"A great book on Hemingway and how he wrote."

"For you?"

"For the shop. I already have a copy."

"It must be good then," she said.

"It explains a lot of Hemingway's writing techniques, " I said and sat back in my chair and let the sun warm my face.

"Have you always written?" she said.

"Not always, but now I can't imagine not writing."

"Does it come easy?"

"It's a process," I said. "An unfolding process. Sometimes that takes time and that's not usually easy."

"How do you know where to start?"

I thought hard about her question and tried to remember what the initial impetus had been for my previous books. The passage of time had taken me far away from the original seeds of those stories, but I remembered how often I thought back on the various events. The more I thought about them the more pieces I remembered and the more incidents I recalled, the more I searched for the connections between them and their collective meaning. What did all the pieces, the various scenes, add up to? What was the significance of the bits of memory? What did the conversations, the string of events driven by desire or as a consequence of something done or said, ultimately mean? Stories have a mystical heritage; they are a lot like dreams that unfold in our conscious life. Some of them are forgotten or never register; others stay with you demanding acknowledgement with just enough mystery and power that you can't let go of them until you unearth their meaning.

"Sometimes you just want to know where the pain or the joy came from," I said, "and the only way to know it is to write the story. Why do you ask?"

"Just curious," she said. "I like to know how things work."

"Thanks for indulging me with the book shops."

"Not a problem," she said. "This is as much your trip as it is mine."

We finished our drinks and walked the short distance back to our apartment. We still had muffulettas left in the refrigerator, and Rose took two quarter slices out onto our patio. We ate a leisurely late afternoon snack and relaxed in the warmth of the day.

"So…are you having a good time?" Rose asked.

"The best," I said. "And you?"

"Of course," she said. "I love this town."

"What is the attraction for you?"

"The energy is different here," she said. "And I feel invisible...in a good way."

"Like not seen?"

"Like an unknown," she said. "Free to be."

"You strike me as someone who has always been free to be."

"That's the way I like it," she said. "I don't want to miss anything."

"I don't see you missing anything you want in your life," I said.

"My life is all about me," she said.

"Any regrets?"

She sipped her coffee and looked away at the lattice wall of colorful bead necklaces.

"Regrets are about the past," she said. "I prefer this moment."

"And now…the moment is New Orleans?"

"I absorb the energy here," she said, "and take it with me when I leave."

"I like the idea of absorbing," I said.

"It's like you and the energy of special places. I feel at home here. And I come back whenever I need the energy."

Rose came over and straddled my legs. She stared straight into my eyes, and I couldn't look away.

"How can I help you?" I said.

"What do you think these are worth, Mr. Bookman?" She cupped her breasts and shook them at me like a burlesque dancer.

"Well…I couldn't really say without seeing what we're talking about."

"Oh they're fine, Mr. Bookman."

"I'm sure they are," I said, "but I can't appraise anything without an examination."

"Then what?"

"Condition, ma'am. Condition is everything."

"I bet it is. Here," she said, slipping my hand under her sweater. "What do you think now?"

"They feel great, but seeing is believing, lady."

"Well, then."

She pulled her sweater off over her head, and I cautiously looked up at the walkway above us for anyone looking down.

Rose didn't look away; she just stared into my eyes. "So what do you think Bookman?"

"Priceless."

She bent down and kissed me. "Why don't you look for that tattoo, Mr. Bookman."

Chapter Twenty

"Fact is made secondary [in New Orleans]
to the desire to live, to love,
and to understand life."
- Sherwood Anderson

At five o'clock, Rose and I caught a cab to Marian and Mike's apartment in the Marigny District. We found them sitting on the large front porch having drinks with their landlord who had the adjoining shotgun apartment. Their landlord was a short man in his forties and very amiable; his wife immediately welcomed us with the offer of a frosty drink. People slowly streamed by in small groups, intermingled with large families making their way down Frenchman Street. The landlord's wife said she had prepared a large tote bag with her special Mardi Gras beverage, plastic cups and bottles of water for our group.

Mike brought us our drinks, and Marian gave Rose and me a quick tour. The apartment was huge compared to our small room and felt like a home. There were two bedrooms, a large kitchen and a nice living room with a big screen TV.

"You guys could've stayed here," Marian said. "God knows there's enough room."

"I really wanted to be in the Quarter," Rose said.

"So what's your place like?" Marian asked. "Is it nice?"

Rose looked over at me. "It's very functional," I said.

"It's perfect for us," she said, "because we haven't been there much."

"We were out all day today," I said. "We just grabbed a quick bite there before coming here."

"I did ask him for an appraisal," Rose said.

"Ha!" Marian said. "What did that entail?"

"Examining her assets," I said. "I'm a trained professional in that area."

We finished our drinks then rejoined their landlord on the front porch. As a group, we slowly made our way toward Franklin Street where the parade was to begin, and the closer we got to the starting point, the more festively-attired people we encountered. Thousands of people of all ages were making their way from all the side streets to their favorite viewing areas. Many of them wore costumes or masks of all descriptions with beads draped around their necks. The parade route was a huge outdoor party that ran all the way back to the French Quarter. Marian came fully prepared having packed beads and a couple of masks in her luggage. Rose had brought a small supply of beads for us which we quickly put on.

Several Krewe parades occur during Mardi Gras, each in a different neighborhood, but the Krewe du Vieux is the first of the season and considered the most individualistic. The theme of the 2015 parade was “Begs for Change” which seemed appropriate on several levels. In 2006, the KdV was the first parade to march post-Katrina and was acknowledged for its tenacity and lightheartedness in the wake of the hurricane. The KdV is known for its wild satire, political commentary and of course adult themes. It also features some of the best local marching bands.

As darkness fell, the crowd closest to the actual starting point of the parade sent out waves of cheers that grew louder in intensity as people further down the parade route added their voices to the roar of anticipation. The excitement intensified as the crowd got louder and more people squeezed in along the route. Excited children ran up and down the street and people with chairs crowded along the curb and sidewalk. Horns blasted, followed by whistles and a growing clamor from the crowd. Finally a blaring roar of trombones and tubas followed by the rolling thunder of drums signaled the first of the traditional human-drawn floats.

For the next hour, a steady stream of more than a dozen floats poked fun at local and national figures and social issues, without subtlety. There was a float devoted to teachers of questionable moral character, one dealing with gay marriage called "50 States of Gay," and another addressing marijuana issues entitled "Toke of the Town." Rose and I stood with Marian's landlords and drank their special Mardi Gras concoction behind the crowds that lined the street, ten-people deep. People were waving, cheering and calling out for beads or any of the handmade items the float riders were tossing out.

The parade was a vibrant display of creativity and imagination that took the various sub-Krewes a year to prepare for. Thousands of people from all over the greater New Orleans area lined the route from the Marigny District back into the Quarter to see what outrageous creations would appear. Following the lead float, the first-line brass band injected many in the crowd with the desire to shimmy in place followed by more than fifteen other brass bands. Once the fleet of floats passed, the second-line bands marked the end of the official entries. Onlookers immediately joined the second-line and danced behind the procession. The distinctive blare of trumpets, the roar of trombones, and the deep-throated thump of tubas announced that if the spirits moved you it was time to join the festivities. Many people waitcd for the second line so they could join the rolling excitement of the music with their own wild, strutting dance moves, some twirling parasols and those without umbrellas flashing white handkerchiefs in time with the slow shuffle of the music.

Mike and Marian joined the second-line while Rose and I strolled along with our drinks. We followed the procession for a couple of blocks, and then stopped in front of a vacant doorway as the last of the strutters passed by.

"So did you like it?" Rose asked.

"Loved it," I said.

"Favorite part?"

"The 'Drip and Discharges' float was pretty fun."

"I liked the 'Spank Squad' myself," Rose said.

"The music was the best. Not something you hear anywhere else."

"I thought you'd like that," she said.

I backed Rose into the dark doorway and kissed her as if we were alone in our room. I didn't let go of her until Marian's voice broke the moment.

"There you guys are," Marian said, stepping into the doorway.

"You two need to get a room," Mike added.

"We were aroused by the music," I said.

"Are you through dancing?" Rose said, stepping away from me.

"God that was fun," Marian said. "I've been waiting all year to do that. So now what?"

"I need a drink," Rose said. "Maybe two."

Chapter Twenty-One

"Heartbreak makes me Horny."
- Graffiti

The Lost Love Lounge was a neighborhood bar, not far from the parade route, that catered to a large local clientele. The bar was packed with the after- parade crowd when we walked in. A party of four was just leaving and we settled in at their table for a post-parade assessment. We ordered a round of drinks while Mike laid out his bag of booty on the table. He had beads, blue and green plastic coins, wrapped candy, a whistle, a button with a tittie on it and a condom.

"All I got was a wooden nickel," I said, and set it on the table.

"Did anyone see a coconut?" Marian asked.

"I didn't," I said.

"I believe they're just in the Zulu parade," Rose said.

Our drinks arrived and, before we could toast the evening, a young woman approached our table and handed me a tin *fleur du lis* keychain with a yellow card attached with a ribbon. The card read the young woman was deaf and would appreciate anything I could spare for the keychain. At first I was reluctant to fall for one of the oldest bar hustles, but Rose was open to the soft touch and took a few dollars from her purse and handed it to the young woman. The woman smiled and pursed her lips in gratitude.

I was shamed into taking the keychain and gave the woman three more dollars.

"Don't you feel better?" Rose said.

"I've seen that in bars all over," I said.

"I'm sure she needs it," Rose said. "You're doing something good. Think of it as a small penance for anything bad you've done."

"Like karma?" I said.

"She'll remember your kindness," Rose said.

"You're full of surprises," I said.

"I hate being predictable," she said.

"That's for sure," Marian said.

"Thank you," Rose said, and excused herself to the ladies room. Marian led us in a toast to an exciting parade, and we shared our favorite parade moments.

When Rose returned from the restroom, she had a big smile on her face.

"You won't believe what was written on the ladies room wall," she said.

"Your name and phone number?" I said.

"Somebody wrote, 'Heartbreak makes me horny.'"

"I love it," Marian said.

"That's a great line," I said.

"Isn't that perfect?" Rose said.

"Too good," I said.

"Think about it," Rose said. "It's so true. I've been heartbroken this whole trip."

"I have to use it," I said. "It's too good not to use in a song."

"Oh yeah," Marian said. "Could be a great blues song."

"I don't know about a song," I said, "but it's certainly a great line."

We finished our drinks and Marian and Mike were ready to call it a night. They were not far from their rental, and we said our 'goodbyes.' Rose and I grabbed a cab and headed for Frenchman Street.

We found Joanie and Jimmy waiting inside the Cajun Diner, known for its Cajun burgers loaded with cayenne pepper and sweet paprika. We were all hungry and got a booth. Rose's friends were good down-home people who both loved music. I liked them the moment I met them the night before at the Blue Nile.

"Rose tells me you're a musician," Joanie said.

"I am."

"So what do you play?" Joanie asked.

"Guitar and sing."

"Musical preference?"

"The blues," I said, "but I like anything played well."

"I love the blues," Joanie said.

"He also writes music," Rose said. "Good songs."

"Well, you guys have to come see us," Joanie said.

"We'll make some music," Jimmy said. "I have lots of musician friends."

I looked over at Rose. "That would be nice," I said.

"I have all kinds of instruments at the house," Jimmy said. "It wouldn't be hard to get some players together."

"And we're just a few hours from here," Joanie said.

"I'd like to see some of the deep south," I said.

"We're good people who love good music," Joanie said.

"It could be a nice trip," Rose said. "Nashville, Memphis."

"I'd also like to see the Delta region of Mississippi," I said. "So much of the music and musicians I like came out of that area. I'd like to see it, smell the air. See what it was that inspired such great music."

"That could happen," Rose said.

"And come see us," Joanie said.

"We'll put you guys up," Jimmy said, "and feed you."

Our Cajun burgers arrived and they were tasty with just enough hot sauce to fix them in your permanent memory. While Rose and Joanie caught up, Jimmy and I talked music. They were both very welcoming and the conversation was easy. We talked and drank until we were all showing signs of wearing down.

"Our new apartment is just two blocks from here," Joanie said. "Come on, let's take a look."

We walked for what seemed like half an hour trying to find their apartment, getting lost in the circular streets that neither Jimmy nor Joanie could remember. Finally we found the right building and got a sneak look at their unfurnished city nest.

"Just let me know if you're coming down," Joanie said, as we were leaving. "We might be able to work the schedule so you have a place to stay."

For Rose and me, it had been a long and well-travelled day. Throw in the drinks, a bit of the herb and all the walking we had done, and the day finally caught up with us. We said our goodbyes and made tentative plans to visit them in the near future.

Rose and I took a cab back to the Quarter where crowds of people continued to wander the streets. Access to Royal Street was still blocked because of the parade route so we exited the cab two blocks from our building. Bourbon Street proper and the sidewalks were littered ankle deep with confetti, broken strands of beads, empty beer bottles and plastic cups. The KdV was the only parade allowed through the Quarter because all the floats had to be propelled by hand. Bourbon Street looked like it had been hit by a tornado, and I couldn't imagine how long it would take to clean it. As far as you could see in any direction, there was trash and debris.

"It'll be clean by morning," Rose said.

"You're kidding me."

"They'll work through the night," she said, "and by morning none of this will be here."

"Everything gone?"

"All of it," she said.

I removed two strands of red beads draped over a fire hydrant and, with a dash of pomp and reverence, draped one around Rose's neck and the other around mine.

"I christen you my Queen of the Krewe du Veaux."

"I accept, *El Presidente*."

When we got back to our modest room, the Quarter and all its festivities dissipated beyond our walls. Despite our proximity to Bourbon Street and all the remaining revelers, our little room was free of the outside noise.

We got into bed and while my body was tired my head was still humming with all the sights and sounds of the day. The faces of the newlyweds we encountered dressed in white and pink danced in my head, as did the image I had of Faulkner writing in his tiny apartment on Pirate's Alley. The hypnotic rhythm of barking tubas, ringing whistles and staccato drums still echoed inside me; I could still see Joanie's expressive face as she talked about singing, and feel the passion in Rose's kisses along the parade route.

I turned to Rose and wrapped my arm around her.

"Today was a great day," I said.

"I'm glad you had a good time."

"I did," I said, "and I like your friends."

"They're good people, and Joanie's a great singer."

"What does she sing?"

"Everything, but not so much anymore. Her lungs aren't what they used to be. I worry about her."

"If they're examples of Southern hospitality, I love it."

"I've known Joanie for years," Rose said. "We've shared a lot of good times."

"Here in New Orleans?"

"And Mississippi. Joanie was playing at a club in Pascagoula. I was with a man named Ben and the three of us had a lot of fun."

"What happened with Ben?"

"We got married and he helped me start my chocolate business in Seattle."

"Where's he now?" I asked.

"He died of a heart attack."

"Like Bob," I said.

"The important thing is Joanie and Jimmy like you."

"Well," I said, "what's not to like?"

"Let's see…your detective work."

"My what?"

"Have you found the tattoo yet?"

"I keep looking, but it seems to be well hidden."

"You're not looking hard enough," she said.

"I'm doing my best," I said.

"Stay focused," she said. "It's there, you just have to find it."

"I'm not sure what I'm looking for," I said.

"You'll know it when you find it."

"You haven't told me what it looks like."

She paused for a moment. "It looks like you," she said.

"Me?"

"Yeah, it looks like you."

"Balding…with a beard?"

"You might have to go deeper," she said.

"Deeper."

"Yes, deeper if you want to find it."

She reached over and turned off the bed lamp.

"How am I supposed to find it in the dark?" I said.

"You don't need a lamp to find what you're looking for," she said.

Chapter Twenty-Two

"I'm fluent in bullshit."
- Rose

The following day was Super Bowl Sunday and our focus for the day was watching the Seattle Seahawks in the Big Game. We got up late and walked up to Bourbon Street for breakfast. To my surprise, the streets were completely cleared of trash and the remnants of the previous night's festivities. After breakfast we made our way to a bar we had passed the day before called Ryan's Irish Pub on Decatur Street. Rose wore her Seahawks T-shirt, and I had on a bead necklace with a plastic Seahawk logo attached to it that Marian loaned me.

A rather large man was sitting at the end of the bar and we took the two available seats next to him with a good view of the big screen. He was a portly fellow dressed in slacks, sports coat and a polo shirt. He was clean shaven with a thin head of hair and a hairline that receded. He looked at Rose sitting next to him and just as the game got underway he engaged her.

"So where you folks from?" he asked Rose.

"Near Seattle," she said.

"And you're here for the game?"

"Just here for fun," Rose said.

"Should be a good game," the man said. "So what do you do up north little lady?"

Without a moment's pause, she said, "I raise chickens and grow pot."

"Damn," he said. "You are a bold one."

"My man here is a musician," she said.

"I get it," he said. "Bohemians. Well, you came to the right town."

"And what do you do?" Rose asked.

"I'm in the agriculture business," he replied.

Rose looked at his attire and then down at his hands.

"You don't look like a farmer," she said.

"Chemicals," he said. "I sell chemicals to farmers."

"And you're here alone?" Rose said.

"I needed a weekend away," he said. "New Orleans seemed like a good place to be this weekend."

"I'm sure you'll have a good time," Rose said.

"Hey Barkeep," the man yelled out. "I'm buying these folks a round."

"That's not necessary," I said.

"I insist," the man said.

The game got underway, and the Seahawks had their hands full from the outset. As good as our team had been, they were not the dominating team we had expected to see. We were the only Seattle fans in the bar, but the opposition crowd never held that against us.

The man next to us wasn't that interested in the game and spent his time trying to engage Rose. Rose was so easy around people she could have conversed with the devil and walked away with his horns. I watched the game, but kept my ears open to the bits of conversation going on next to me.

"I'm sure your wife would love to hear from you regardless," I heard Rose say.

"I didn't come here to talk to her," he said.

"That's a shame," she said. "You should be more respectful."

"If you'll excuse me, young lady," the man said and he headed for the restroom.

"What was that all about?" I said.

"He's just being a jerk," she said.

"You want to go somewhere else?'

"No," she said. "I like this place."

"Switch places?"

"No, I'm fine."

At halftime we stepped outside for a smoke.

"We can finish the game somewhere else," I said.

"I'm really fine here."

"He's clearly hitting on you."

"Are you worried?"

"Not in the least. I'm just thinking about you."

"I'm just playing with him."

"Is that smart?"

"He's down here cheating on his wife," she said. "He deserves to be messed with."

We went back inside for the second half and took our seats at the bar. Chemical Man continued his play on Rose, and I could hear her stringing him along. Finally as the third quarter started, I heard Chemical Man whisper something I couldn't hear.

Rose replied with, "Thanks, but no thanks."

"Are you sure?" he said.

"Quite," she said.

"I think that's enough," I finally said to him.

"It's okay," Rose said to me. "He's said all he's going to say. Besides," she said, turning back to Chemical Man, "I'm going to fuck my man tonight, and you should go home to your wife."

"Maybe you misunderstood me," he said.

"No," she said, "I heard you. But the truth is…I'm fluent in bullshit."

Chemical Man looked stunned and leaned back away from Rose. He threw back the rest of his drink, laid a nice tip on the bar, and then left.

"That was well played," I said.

"I don't like cheats," she said.

We ordered two more of Ryan's famous "Irish Car Bombs" and watched the last of the game that turned into a disaster for us Seattleites. With only seconds left in the game, Seattle had first down on the one-yard line for the win. But instead of running the ball they chose to pass which was intercepted on the goal line by the Patriots ending Seattle's chance for back-to-back Super Bowl victories. We stared at the screen with disbelief and no amount of alcohol made the outcome better.

After the game, we took a leisurely stroll around the Quarter trying to walk-off the Seahawk's devastating loss. We grabbed a light dinner at a bar featuring a tight R&B group then slowly made our way back to our room. We sat outside under a dry, clear sky, and I thought about the way Rose handled Chemical Man and her displeasure with a man looking to cheat on his wife.

"Was it the cheating," I asked, "or him?"

"He's free to do what he wants," she said, "but not with me. That changed things."

"Why?"

"It got personal," she said.

We sat there in the quiet of the evening and smoked our way to a more comfortable place, before we loved each other late into the night.

Chapter Twenty-Three

"When we visit sacred sites, we ... perform our acts of respect and then see what happens."
- James Swan, Ethnographer

Place is the tissue that ties events to people and their actions. Place reflects human temperament and the relationship between what is far away and what is near. When we have long forgotten names and no longer recognize faces, the power of place is still remembered. Place is where memory resides. There are beautiful places where lives have flourished, and there are shadowed places where lives have gone wrong. The longer we live the more we realize we can return to places, revisit the past, speak with the dead, address our lost self…that part of us that disappeared at some point…and if we're lucky enough, we understand what happened there.

The events surrounding President Kennedy's assassination happened more than fifty years ago yet the cities involved, the streets on which players walked, the places where they ate, the rooms where decisions were made remain a part of history. Buildings may change, but the spirit of what occurs in a place endures.

Monday was our last full day in New Orleans and the final thing I wanted to do was visit the place where some of the suspected participants in the JFK assassination had plotted their involvement. Rose and I caught a bus to Lafayette Square which sits right in the middle of the legal district south of Canal Street. The bus dropped us off two blocks from the square and for a Monday the streets were surprisingly quiet.

Some of the New Orleans underworld involved in the Kennedy assassination and other covert activities congregated and conducted their criminal activities in the office of a man named Guy Banister. Banister was a retired New Orleans police officer and former employee of the FBI. He was known to be a key liaison for a number of U.S. government-sponsored anti-Communist activities. In 1963, Banister's private investigation office was in what was at the time the Newman Building at 531 Lafayette Street. Around the corner in the same building, but with an entrance on

544 Camp Street, were the upstairs offices of the Fair Play for Cuba organization; the same group accused assassin Lee Harvey Oswald distributed leaflets for the summer before Kennedy was shot. Banister's office was also two blocks from the Reily Coffee Company which had reported affiliations with CIA operatives. It was also where Oswald worked briefly, up until four months before the assassination.

Outside of Dealey Plaza in Dallas, Lafayette Square was for me the second-most important intersection connected to the assassination. Rose and I had talked about the significance of this place before we got to New Orleans. I was especially intrigued by the fact the southern regional Office of Naval Intelligence, the FBI, the CIA and the Secret Service were all located in the government building facing Lafayette Square. Lafayette Square was across the street from Banister's office, and two blocks from the Reily Coffee Company. For half an hour, we tried to find Banister's office building at 531 Lafayette Street, but to no avail. We found the corner of Lafayette and Camp Streets, but Banister's address in a Newman Building no longer existed. It wasn't until we got home that I learned the Newman Building had been torn down in 1972 and replaced, ironically, with the Hale Boggs Federal Building and U.S. Court House. Congressman Boggs was one of three dissenting members of the Warren Commission who doubted Oswald was the lone killer. Boggs died in a mysterious plane crash in 1972.

For the assassination of the President to be successful, highly-placed people had to control the disposition of the Secret Service, the FBI agents in Dallas, and ensure the required military protection for a visiting President was canceled. A lone, "disgruntled," ex-marine private would not have the authority to direct any one of those agencies let alone all of them.

Rose and I sat down on a bench near the bronze plaque of the Hungarian revolutionary Louis Kossuth and quietly took in the large government complex around us. Straight ahead, across the park, would have been Banister's office at the corner of Camp and Lafayette Streets.

"So all those agencies were right here?" Rose said.

"And right across the street were some of the plotters."

"But they didn't actually do it," she said.

"Not directly," I said, "but they made arrangements. People at the top made decisions. People who could control the activities of the FBI, the

CIA, the Secret Service and the military. That's where it gets scary."

We sat there for a while and let the scene sink in. The square was quiet except for a few lone walkers and several women pushing strollers; but some bad things occurred around this tree-lined park where young mothers, living the American dream, were playing with their children. There was a darkness to what transpired here in the summer of 1963 that led to the killing of the president four months later. If the president wasn't safe, then none of us are; and if we aren't safe from our own government our American way of life is a lie.

"So what's the answer?" Rose said, looking around the park.

I turned to her, staring at the side of her face while I gave serious thought to her question. "People in high places..," I started to say. "People in high places, people in our government, had the President killed."

Rose looked over at me. "Maybe there are things we shouldn't know," she said. "Maybe we just live our lives. We grow pot, raise chickens and make music."

"Maybe we're the dinosaurs," I said. "Simple creatures that don't see the end game."

"And...what is the end game?"

"Bad people in power get the world they want at any cost," I said. "Remember our conversation about assets? Well, a lot of assets were needed for the war in Vietnam that some powerful people wanted."

Rose watched a small boy running on the grass next to his mother, and then stared straight ahead.

"It's hard to comprehend," she said. "It's such a peaceful place."

I focused my eyes on a woman sitting not far from us on a bench, flipping through her phone. She had her back to her daughter who was talking to her doll as though her mother wasn't present.

"It fractured us," I said.

Rose looked over at me. "It what?"

"Fractured us."

"In what way?"

"It destroyed our faith in the government… in other people. It shattered everything"

"Not everything."

"Everything important," I said. "The taboo was broken and, when you eat your own, it can break you so you're never the same."

We sat quietly on the bench next to the plaque of my fellow Hungarian Louis Kossuth amidst the sounds of happy children.

"What does anything mean, then?"

I looked to my right at the massive concrete Federal building that hid the light of the sun.

"I'm not sure," I said. "Once something is broken, it's never the same again. So many things are broken, and there is no fixing them."

"Are you sure?"

"I wish I wasn't," I said.

"Maybe we just embrace what is right in our life."

Despite everything I knew about what had happened around this place and in Dallas, the event couldn't be changed. The damage had been done, and we lived with the consequences. For me, just confirming this park existed and knowing all the investigative work that had been done placing conspirators in and around this place was enough for me.

"It's kind of depressing," Rose said.

"It just makes me appreciate what is good in my life ," I said.

"I like that," she said. "How about some lunch?"

Mother's Restaurant was two blocks from Lafayette Square and the lunch crowd was already lined up outside. The diner was known for their chicken and ham dinners and had a long history going back to the 1930s. I couldn't help wondering how many of the plotters had eaten at Mother's and ordered the same lunches we did.

Rose suggested we grab a trolley and see the Garden District. We both got po'boys to go and ate lunch in the park. After lunch, we caught a trolley and rode from the commercial district through a more residential neighborhood where large white estates dating back to the early 1900's lined the street. As we rolled past pillared mansions, some under various stages of renovation, with lush gardens and long circular driveways, I was struck by the powerful places in the different neighborhoods. We passed Tulane and Loyola Universities and more stately homes of the wealthiest of New Orleans. This was the moneyed part of the city, the Beverly Hills of New Orleans, and not that far from Lafayette Square.

We took the trolley back into town and at Canal Street we got off and walked along the levee.

"Thanks for indulging me with Lafayette Square," I said.

"It was very informative," Rose said. "I would not have known to go there or known what had happened around there."

"I needed to see it myself," I said, "to know it was real."

"And now that you know the place is real?" Rose asked.

"It makes belief in other things easier," I said.

"Like what?" Rose said.

"I know how I feel about you," I said, "and I know that is real."

The wind off the river was bitter cold, and we agreed to walk back into the Quarter. We strolled up to the west end of Royal Street and took in the part of our street we hadn't previously walked. There were more high-end shops and galleries that catered to a different clientele than our end of Royal. One shop caught my attention with a window display of Civil War swords, a set of leather-bound books and a vintage guitar. We went inside and I saw they had a glass display case with a lot of nice autographed books. The shop also had an area of music-related collectibles including signed photographs. I looked at the signed items and roamed around hoping to find something I could make money on, but everything was priced at high retail. I found Rose looking in the glass cases at the front of the store with coins, jewelry, and documents. We left without a purchase, but it was nice to see some very unique items even if I couldn't make any money on them.

When we got back to our room, instead of going out to eat, we finished off our remaining muffulettas and brewed up two Happy Coffees. We sat out on our patio and enjoyed the quiet and being still without any more stimuli. For me, the stillness allowed me to process all I had experienced in the short time we had been in New Orleans. But there was more to our getaway than just the sights and the sounds. The events were just the backdrop against which my time with Rose could be measured. And for the first time in a long time, I was not just pleased, but so completely at ease and appreciative that Rose was in my life. I had no words to describe how I felt. I didn't know the words for that feeling. It was like an electrical filament connected us on a molecular level. We were so in tune with one another that words were not enough to express what I was feeling. But that didn't stop me from trying to express how I felt.

"This has been the best trip," I said.

"I'm glad," Rose said. "I've had a good time too."

"I feel like I've been transported to some other life. Like I'm learning to be me again. I don't know how else to say it. Thank you for asking me along."

"Hey…Gisele Bundchen wasn't available."

"Who?"

"Gisele Bundchen. A Brazilian model I would bang."

"Well…I'm glad she wasn't available."

"I like being with you too," she said.

"And I like who you are," I said. "You make it easy to enjoy life again."

"I raise dinosaurs and grow pot."

"And serve Happy Coffee."

"You've found my secret."

"I'm resisting climbing all over you right now."

"It's futile, *El Presidente*."

"I'm stronger than you think."

"Bullshit. You want to and you know it." She got out of her chair and came over and straddled my lap.

"You are so very cute and hunky, and I want you right now."

We lay in bed, both of us trying to catch our breath.

"You are trying to kill me," she said.

"I just don't want you to want anyone else," I said. I reached down and touched her.

"Don't…don't" she said. "I can't again. You'll kill me." From outside we could hear the plaintive sound of a lone saxophone echoing up from Royal Street that spun a melodic web over our room.

"I love you madly," I said.

"Of course you do. You just got laid."

"I mean it."

"No, you don't," she said and sat up on the edge of the bed.

I ran my hand down her bare back then pulled her to me. "You mean the world to me, and I want you to know it. I said it because it's true."

She looked at me for a moment, kissed me, and then went into the bathroom. It was hard hearing Rose denying how I felt about her. I wanted her to know how much she meant to me, not just in the bedroom but in my life. I had been in enough relationships and marriages to know how I felt about someone. There are different levels of love and affection, and what I felt for Rose was a level I had not experienced in my sixty-eight years. She was not only beautiful on the outside and sexy, but she had an inner attraction I was constantly drawn to. I felt she knew things about me I needed to know about myself. She allowed me to be me without any strings attached.

"Do you believe things happen for a reason?" I asked her when she returned from the bathroom.

"I'm sure they do," she said.

"I feel like my whole life was in preparation for today."

"What was special about today," she asked.

"Not just today," I said, "but this time in my life."

"What do you think has happened?"

"You," I said.

"I didn't just happen," she said. "I've always been."

"And so have I," I said, "but here we are and life feels completely different."

"We're older," she said, "with things to do."

"I agree," I said, "and part of that is who you do those things with and who you do them for."

"It's all about me," she said.

"I don't believe that," I said.

"I do see things in people, but in the end it's all about me. Just as your life is all about you."

"Right now I'm remembering a woman in my first book who reminds me of you."

"That Mother…something?"

"Motherbright," I said. "Exactly. The similarities are uncanny. It's like I've known you before."

"Like déjà vu?"

"More like bookends in my life. Motherbright when I was eighteen and now you at sixty-eight."

"There is a circle to life," she said.

"I have no idea what it all means," I said, "but it does make me think…you know…about larger things."

We had an early flight the next morning, and I didn't want to say anything more that might disrupt the perfect time we had just shared.

On our Tuesday morning flight home, we were both quiet. For me it was an opportunity to reflect on all that had transpired over the previous four days and think about what lay ahead for us. It had only been four months since we first met, but it felt like I had known Rose long before I met her. I was still leery of jumping to conclusions after such a short period of time, but I knew Rose was not like anyone I had ever known. I was also fully aware that she was a recent widow and I knew very little about her life with Bob. I purposely avoided bringing him up, despite my desire to know as much as I could about her previous life. I was in her life now, and if she wanted me to know anything about him she would tell me. I was more concerned with where we were.

"What are you thinking about?" I asked.

"Just remembering right now," she said. "I've just been remembering."

"About the past or the trip?"

"Both," she said.

"Remembering is good."

"And being remembered for something good."

"So how did we do" I asked.

"On the trip?"

"Yes."

"Good," she said.

"You would tell me if there were any problems?"

"We're good, *El Presidente*. We're good."

Chapter Twenty-Four

"Time is our most valuable asset."
- Rose

We both had to catch up with our island lives after our brief trip to New Orleans. I had books to inventory, online orders to process, and a ton of emails that needed responses. Rose's neighbor Rozie had been taking care of Bella and the chickens but there were dozens of eggs for Rose to clean for the market, fresh treats to bake and meals to make for her Alzheimer's couple.

Valentine's Day was upon us and we both agreed historically it had not been a big event for either of us, but this year felt different. We were in love and still savoring the memories of our trip to New Orleans. Several local venues offered music but it was a Zydeco band playing at the Deer Lagoon Grange Hall, in conjunction with Fat Tuesday, that was our first choice for the evening. We felt it would be a dressy affair so we decided to doll up.

Rose wore her tight-fitting red dress, knee-high boots, black mesh stockings, and one of her finest berets. A pair of feather earrings accented her smile. I wore my black sport coat, black slacks with a white scarf for color. When Rose came out of the bedroom, I was again stunned at how beautiful she looked. She looked great in jeans and rubber boots around the Ranch, but she was a knockout when she put on a dress.

"My God…you are so…I'm speechless," I said, when I saw her.

"Thank you."

"You're beautiful every day, but you have ramped up the sizzle by a factor of ten."

"You look nice too," she said.

"This could be dangerous taking you out looking like this. I'll probably have to kill somebody tonight."

It turned out we were the only couple dressed up in any formal way that night. We stood out like two sore thumbs in an otherwise denim and sweatshirt crowd. We listened to the Cajun music and soaked in the feeling of the night that clearly reminded us of the sounds of New Orleans. Aside from the music, the hall did not have the atmosphere I was looking for. It was the first time in a while I really felt like

Valentine's Day was special, and I didn't want it to end on such a mundane note.

I suggested we take our dressy night out up to Prima Bistro and get a proper drink in a more sophisticated atmosphere. I wanted a nicer setting that better suited how beautiful Rose looked that night.

It was late enough that we easily found a table for two at Prima, and I could feel the eyes from the bar burning holes into us as we seated ourselves.

After we ordered our drinks, I leaned over the table and whispered, "You're turning heads, your ladyship."

"Stop it," Rose said. She lowered her head and looked away from the bar.

"If you don't believe me look around."

"I will not," she whispered back.

"Then trust me," I said, "chins will be wagging."

Rose kept her head down and refused to look around. I took her hand and lowered my head so I could look into her eyes. She slowly looked up, leaned forward, and whispered, "Come closer."

I leaned forward and she kissed me long and hard, cupping her hands around my face and drawing out the kiss.

"Well," she said, "that should do it."

I didn't have to look around to feel the eyes on us. I told her again how beautiful she looked and how much I wanted her right then.

"I have something for you," she said.

"No," I said, "we can't do that here."

She reached into her purse and pulled out a small white box and handed it to me. I opened the box and removed the cushion of white cotton. Inside was a coin with a small eye on it for a chain. I looked at it and flipped it over. One side had some Arabic-looking writing on it and on the other side were the words in English: "East India Company, 1808."

"It reminded me of the conversation we had," she said. "You know…mapping the assets of the world."

"I remember."

"I thought you'd like it," she said.

"I do. Thank you."

"These were uncirculated," she said. "They were aboard a ship that sunk in the English Channel on their way to India."

"Listen to you with all this history," I said.

"You set a high bar," she said.

"Where did you find this?"

"New Orleans."

"But where and when? You and I were together all the time."

"You can think about that," she said.

"I can't imagine when you had the opportunity."

"I'll get you a chain for it," she said. "I just haven't had the time."

"Thank you so much," I said. "It's an interesting slice of history."

"It made me think of us," she said, "and New Orleans."

"How?"

"Mapping our way out in the world."

"New Orleans?" I asked.

"And other possibilities. It just struck me as perfect when I saw it."

I reached into my coat pocket and pulled out a small box of my own and gave it to her.

"This was supposed to be a Christmas present then a birthday gift but I ran into difficulty getting what I wanted."

She opened the box and removed the gold-plated, oval pendant and held it up by the matching gold chain. I had the name "Rose" engraved across the face of the pendant.

"It's beautiful," she said.

"Just like you."

"Thank you so much. This is perfect."

We finished our drinks at Prima and drove back to the Ranch. I walked around and opened her door and offered her my hand.

"He'p me," she said, as she tried to get out of the car, "he'p me." She sounded like a southern belle demurring to a gentleman caller.

I lifted her out of the car and took her in my arms and kissed her. "It was my pleasure being in your company tonight, Miss Rose."

"Oh Beauregard, how you do carry on."

I pressed her against the car, and she wrapped her leg around mine. She reached down and cupped me in her hand and squeezed gently.

"I could hurt you right now," she said.

"But you won't."

"You don't know that," she said.

"You want me too much right now to hurt me."

"I could take care of myself."

"Not like I will," I said, "and you know that."

"What if I needed to hurt you?"

"Why would you need to do that?"

"What if it were necessary?"

"Necessary in what way?"

"To save us from more pain."

I just looked at her unsure where her questions were coming from.

She smiled, pushed me away and we went inside where Bella was eagerly waiting for our return. Rose went into the bedroom while I fed Mr. Kitty and gave

Bella her late night dog bone before turning out the lights.

I helped Rose out of her boots then got out of my clothes. Rose sat on the end of the bed and slowly removed her feather earrings. I crawled into bed and when Rose stood up she slowly slipped out of her dress. She undid her hair, letting it fall around her face, and all she had on was her black mesh stockings. She stood at the foot of the bed looking at me with an impish smile, her hands on her slightly cocked hips.

"You're a sight to behold," I said. "What about the stockings?"

"Oh, they won't be a problem," she said.

"I think they might get in the way."

"If you had been a little more exploratory tonight," she said, "you would know they're open where they need to be." She raised her right leg onto the bed, and even in the room's dim light I could clearly see what she meant.

"You were like that all night, and you didn't say anything?"

"I thought I'd let you find out for yourself," she said. "Like the tattoo."

"I still haven't found that yet," I said.

"You don't know that."

"You could have given me a hint," I said.

"That wouldn't have been as fun."

She slowly crawled onto the bed and pulled the covers back. She straddled me and moved just enough so there was contact but nothing more.

"I'm going to play with you tonight," she said. "Play with you until you beg me to let you in, *El Presidente*."

"I'll beg right now," I said, "to save time."

"Time is our most valuable asset," she said, "but it's not going to be that easy tonight. I want you to remember *this* time," she said as she slowly rocked her body. "I want you to think about what you could have had tonight at the Grange Hall. I don't want you to ever forget me."

Chapter Twenty-Five

"If you find it in your heart to care for somebody else, you will have succeeded."
- Maya Angelou

I was now spending more time at the Ranch than I was at my own apartment. I had some of my clothes there so I wouldn't have to always go home to shower and change and, with all its simplicity, the Ranch felt more like home to me. It was the extreme opposite of the house my ex-wife and I had bought. For all the beauty that house had, sitting on five wooded acres, it never felt like my home. It was a conspicuous statement that turned out to be more than we could afford.

The Ranch was unpretentious, and I enjoyed helping Rose with tasks around the kitchen and with the chickens. When I would spend the night with Rose, which was most every night by now, I would help her in the morning clean eggs or prepare baked goods for the market. I would stay as long as I could before going to the shop, just to savor our time together.

Some mornings there would be an easy conversation about her plans to maximize what she could do with the Ranch; other days we talked about family or music or what we wanted out of life. One morning she told me, she was going to visit her daughter who lived just north of Seattle. Her name was Bethany and she was married with three daughters of her own. I waited for the invite to accompany her, but it didn't come. Rose's lack of family discussion led me to believe there was a lot of distance between her and her daughter. In an earlier conversation she told me, at the age of eighteen, she had given up her daughter to the parents of the father. It was clear there were still family issues over that part of Rose's past. She would visit her daughter and granddaughters on special occasions and bring the girls something special from her closet of colorful and unusual clothing. I didn't press the subject of her daughter, but I could feel there was still a heavy weight hanging over their relationship that was not easily discussed.

As is often the case, it is the things we don't talk about that weigh heaviest on us.

After one of my regular Tuesday night rehearsals with the band, I returned to the Ranch after being away since ten in the morning. When I walked into the house, I immediately saw a difference in the small living room.

"What have you done?" I said.

"I bought some new furniture," she said.

"I guess you did."

Instead of just one easy chair, there was now a second chair with a small table between the two. And the old Camelback sofa, usually occupied by Bella, had been replaced by a new fiery red sleeper sofa.

"So what do you think?" Rose said.

"I think you have a very comfortable living room now."

"Comfortable for two," she said. "You won't have to sit by yourself on Bella's couch."

"I like it," I said.

"This is the most money I've ever spent on furniture in my life," she said. "But it's worth it. Now we each have a chair and if someone visits, we have a fold-out bed."

I had been working at my second job at the grocery store for over a year and a half and it was starting to bring me down. I had needed the extra income to pay off lingering debts from my marriage, but I had reached the point where the modestly paying job was not making up for the customers I had to deal with. I knew some people on the island lived very modest lives and others had substance issues, but to see the ongoing parade of people with bad hygiene and others who ate poorly was hard to take on a daily basis. I also couldn't make any long-term plans because the shift schedules were made only a week in advance with no consistency in my days off. Booking music gigs was getting more complicated, and my usual two to eight p.m. shift was cutting into the life I was trying to build with Rose.

"I don't know how much longer I can work at the grocery," I told Rose one morning.

"Then you should quit," she said. "Do you still need the money?"

"I'm close to catching up."

"But you're unhappy," she said.

"Just when I'm there."

"You don't have to do it," she said. "Life's too short. You have the book shop and your music."

Rose made it all sound so easy.

"You should go on more buying trips," she said. "I could be in the shop while you're gone."

"Really?"

"I've done retail and I'm good with people."

"You would do that?" I said. "Along with everything else you do?"

"I could do that for you."

She reminded me of her chocolate business and said she could make the time.

"And you should write more music," she said. "I like the songs you've written. You should write more."

"I wish it were that easy," I said. "Most of what I've written was out of frustration and anger. A hard marriage will do that."

"But you chose to stay," she said.

"I kept hoping it would get better," I said, "but you can't change who someone is. And things never got better."

"Now you've walked away."

"I'm not happy it failed," I said, "but the longer we stayed together the further apart we grew. Then I got sick. We had been separated for a few months when I was told they wanted me to start chemo therapy."

"And now?"

"I'm divorced and three years clear."

"Cured?"

"There is no cure, but there is treatment. It's not a problem, trust me."

"Of course it's a problem."

"It's a problem like your heart condition," I said. "It's there, but there are ways to live with it."

I could tell she was concerned; the word cancer will do that. I was concerned when I got the diagnosis. But for some reason I wasn't afraid of the cancer. I had cancer and my oncologist prescribed a treatment. I underwent the chemo and so far I was clear. I had cancer for a reason but neither I nor my doctor could say why or where it came from. Perhaps it was to challenge me, to see if I would fall apart. My attitude was, if it's fatal so be it; if not maybe I'll be stronger because of it.

"I have an oncology appointment coming up," I said. "I want you to come with me. Hear for yourself what my doctor says. You can ask him anything you want. I don't want you worrying about me dying on you."

As soon as the words left my mouth, I realized I had done what I wanted most to avoid—bring up the death of a loved one. But I could sense her reservations about my health, and I didn't want that to affect our future.

"I didn't mean for it to come out that way," I said. "I just want you to know it's not as serious as it sounds."

"It is a serious thing," she said, "but I'll do that. I'll go with you."

Chapter Twenty-Six

"The Spirits Fly."
- Cherub

We had been back from New Orleans three weeks when the woman I considered my unofficial spiritual advisor came by the shop to see how I was doing after the divorce.

Cherub was not her given name, but the name she had adopted and all of her friends on the island knew her by. The name also suited her personality. It was hard not to love her. She had a large presence and an infectious positive spirit. No matter what was going on in someone's life, she always saw a silver lining in a problem. She would inject a positive remedy that at times struck me as a bit unconventional. When she learned I had leukemia, she immediately came to see me and insisted I do a cleanse and go on a juicing regimen for a month. As foreign and dubious as her treatment struck me, I was willing to take her advice and in the end, felt better for it.

I got to know Cherub through my ex-wife after I moved to the island. Cherub was a serious and knowledgeable practitioner of the spiritual arts. She was well-versed in herbalism, the use of natural oils, and the divinity of the individual. She had studied with shamans, Native American healers and a variety of celestial-art practitioners. She had a natural remedy for almost every physical and emotional condition. Her life-calling was totally foreign to me, but she was a good human being, knowledgeable, and I loved her for her enthusiasm and positive attitude.

While I was not an immediate acolyte of Cherub's belief system, I was not one to denigrate how she viewed the world or her approach to living as wholesomely as possible. I always listened to the experiences she shared with me and never doubted the positive effect they had on her life. So whenever I saw her, I was open to her unique perspective on life and living well.

The day she stopped by the shop, she asked how my life was with the divorce, and I unhesitatingly told her I was in love with the most wonderful woman in the world.

"I'm so happy for you," she said. "Who is she?"

"No one you know," I said. I gave her a thumbnail sketch of Rose and Cherub could clearly see how happy I was.

"You look like you're in love," she said. "I can see it on you, and the spirits fly."

"I feel better than I have in years."

"You look great," she said. "And business…how are things?"

"A little slow," I said. "I was in New Orleans for a while and it's taking some time to get back up to speed."

"It's been a while since I've been by," she said, "so we should give the shop a blessing." She took my hand, lowered her head, and spoke of bringing wealth and generosity to the shop and continued good health to me. She said a blessing for bringing love into my life and all the pleasures that go with it.

"I have errands," she said, "but I am so happy for your happiness and I bless you for letting love into your heart."

She started for the door, then turned back to me.

"Take a five-dollar bill," she said, "and touch all your books with it."

"A five-dollar bill?" I said.

"It'll wake up the money spirits and you will sell books."

I thanked her for coming by, and told her it was always a special experience seeing her.

"Touch the books," she said, "and I love you."

I closed the shop door behind her and smiled to myself. As foreign as her approach to life was to me, it was hard to dismiss her unapologetic optimism and belief in good things happening if you just ask for them.

I was about to sit down at my computer and then thought—what the hell. What could it hurt? I took a five-dollar bill out of my wallet and started dragging it over the spines of the books in the shop. It took less than ten minutes, and when I finished touching all the books, I got on with my day. The next day a longtime customer, who I hadn't seen in months, came into the shop and spent $2000 on several expensive books. Just when I needed an infusion of cash, there it was. I immediately sent Cherub an email explaining what had happened. I closed with—"Toots, I do believe, thank you."

Chapter Twenty-Seven

"I'll sell eggs, and you'll play music."
- Rose

Rose and I got up early the day of my oncology appointment and fought the commuter traffic to the V.A. hospital on Seattle's Beacon Hill. I went to the lab alone and quickly gave some blood. My oncology appointment was scheduled for 1 p.m. so we used the time in between to run other errands around town. We drove to a nearby restaurant for breakfast, then went to a little Italian grocery in the SODO district and bought a supply of Turkish coffee for our mornings. We drove up to the Pike Place Market and delivered twelve dozen of Rose's eggs to one of her vendors in the market. We bought some donut holes and two coffees and sat where we could people watch.

"Where was your chocolate stand?" I asked.

"Over in the craft section," she said. "I really liked being here."

"I used to come here all the time," I said. "Sorry to say I don't recall seeing you."

"You probably weren't looking for chocolates."

"When I lived downtown, I liked to come here and have lunch and listen to the street musicians. I loved the Athenian Café and Lowell's."

"I worked at the Athenian," Rose said.

"You're kidding."

"I was a waitress. I loved working there. The most interesting characters came through there."

"I did several interviews there."

"With who?" she said

"Mostly jazz players who were in town. I wrote on entertainment for the university newspaper, and I'd meet musicians here. They loved the market."

"I hated giving up my space here."

"Speaking of space…what did the dairy woman say about your eggs?"

"She said she could sell all the eggs I could deliver."

"That sounds good."

"But I already sell all I have," she said.

"How about expanding?" I said. "Get more hens."

"Perhaps if I doubled my hens, I could deliver here twice a week. Nobody else sells natural eggs at the market."

"Even better."

"I've even thought about opening an egg stand here. I could sell at retail instead of wholesale."

"That could work."

"Let's go down to the office as long as we're here," she said, "and see what's available."

The young woman in the market office handed Rose the paperwork for vendors and confirmed no one else directly sold farm fresh eggs in the market and it would be perfect for their needs.

"Could we also have the paperwork for musicians?"

"Buskers? Sure."

Rose turned to me. "We might as well see about you playing here. I think there's a small fee."

"Yes," the young woman said. "It's $30 a year to play."

I took the paperwork and we made our way back to the car.

"So what are you thinking?" I asked.

"I'll sell eggs and you'll play music."

"By myself?"

"You'll do well," she said. "There are a lot of players here, but you would do fine."

"So we would come into town…?"

"…a few days a week," she said. "I would sell eggs and you would play the street."

"And twice as many hens are doable?"

"All I have to do is order them. It would take a while before they were producing, so we're looking at next summer."

"Let's think about this," I said, "and see what we can do."

"I love the market," she said. "It would be nice to live down here."

"Like a second home?"

"It's a thought."

We drove back to the V.A., and at 1 p.m. my name was called. Rose and I followed my oncologist into an examining room. I introduced Rose to my doctor and told him I wanted her to hear from him about my condition.

"Well, your blood work looks good," he said. "Your levels are all normal, right where we want them. How are you feeling?"

"Great," I said. "Never better. I'm in good company. Could you repeat what you've told me about treatments if it returns?"

"Like I told you, this is a chronic disease. There's a chance it will return but we have new treatments today that are more effective and less caustic than what you were given last time."

At my request, he explained exactly the type of leukemia I had so Rose would hear it directly from the doctor. She asked a couple of questions and once she heard what she needed to hear, the appointment was over for another six months.

"So, are you okay with everything?" I said on the way back to the car.

"He was very clear," she said.

"I wanted you to hear it straight from the doctor, in case you thought I was blowing smoke."

"No," she said, "I believe you."

"I don't want you to worry, okay. Because, I'm fine with this. If it comes back, I'll deal with it. I'm not going anywhere."

"I'm fine," she said. "I'm fine."

Chapter Twenty-Eight

"I WAS THINKING WE WOULD OPEN A BAR."
- ROSE

Two days after my oncology appointment I informed Rose: "I gave my two week notice at the grocery store." She was finishing her baking for the evening when I got to the Ranch at 8:30 p.m.

"That's great," she said. "You don't need it anymore."

"It just isn't fun anymore or profitable. I couldn't take another visit from the smelly people or the crackheads getting another sugar fix."

"I'm happy," she said. "You have things to do."

I had been thinking how much time I spent at the Ranch versus the little time I spent at my apartment. We were clearly getting along fine and there were no problems of compatibility. We enjoyed each other's company, and I liked being at the Ranch. She was working with her lawyer about getting legal ownership of the property and dealing with Bob's estranged daughter's claim to a settlement.

I checked in with Rose as to how she felt we were doing and once again she said: "Good. We're fine."

"Are you sure?"

"Positive."

"Well given how much time I'm here, it seems a waste of money for me to keep the apartment."

"And…?"

"Some of that money could offset Ranch expenses and I would save a little money."

"Well…."

"Unless that wouldn't work for you."

"No, it's not that."

"Too soon?"

"I'm just thinking about space," she said. "Where we'd put your things."

"I don't have that much," I said. "Some clothes, a couple guitars, and a chest of drawers. That's about it."

"I suppose I could consolidate," she said. "Go through my closet. There are things I no longer wear."

"All I'd need is a couple of drawers and a little closet space. Some of my clothes are already here."

"I'll see what I can do," she said.

The following day when I returned from the shop, Rose was in the kitchen packing up dinners for her Alzheimer's couple.

"Lucy…I'm home," I called out from the front door.

"Hey Desi."

She stopped what she was doing and grabbed me by the arm.

"Come and take a look," she said.

I followed her to the rear of the house and the walk-in closet area.

"I made room here in the closet for you, and the top two drawers in this chest can be yours."

She opened her antique armoire and there was enough room for my heavy coats.

"Is this going to be enough room?" she asked.

"More than enough," I said.

"Are you sure? If you need more…."

"No this will be fine. Thank you. You've been busy."

"I had some clothes I haven't worn in years and probably never will again. We can put your chest in the living room. I made some space in the bathroom too."

I took her in my arms and kissed her. "I love it here," I said, "and I love you madly."

"No you don't," she said. "Now let me get back to work. I have to see my Alzheimer's."

I looked at the space she had made for me in the closet and the plastic bags full of her discards, and I felt like I was home.

The following day, I gave notice to my landlady and began moving my modest possessions to the Ranch. By Tax Day I was officially part of the Welcome Road Krewe for which there was no medallion, but it felt just as special.

Spring was the perfect time for making plans. We talked about raising the visibility of the market with some social media and expanding the menu. The one dish I was best at preparing was a rich Bolognese sauce that Rose liked. She suggested we grow our own tomatoes and spices and offer my sauce in the market. That weekend, we went to a local nursery and bought a dozen tomato plants, some Italian herbs, and several bell pepper starts. I had not been interested in gardening in my previous life, but this was a joint effort I took to immediately. Rose had two raised planter beds in the front yard that had not been tended to in some time and a lot of large empty plastic pots.

We cleaned up the planters and mixed in some fertilizer and several bags of potting soil. We planted six of the tomato plants in one of the raised beds along with the peppers and various Italian herbs. We put the remaining plants in six large plastic containers and set them on the front deck where they would get full summer sun. I felt invigorated weeding the planters and preparing the fresh dirt with nutrients, then planting baby starts and seeds in the barren ground. I couldn't wait for the plants to take root and the seeds to sprout. From that moment on, every day on the Ranch took on a new sense of growth and renewal.

Rose didn't have cable television but she did have a Smart TV which gave us access to all the premium channels and the internet. She suggested we watch the HBO series "*Treme*" together because of its New Orleans setting. We watched all four seasons and it was very good. We constantly pointed out places we had visited and people we had heard play. There were scenes at the Spotted Cat as well as several performances shot at the Blue Nile featuring Kermit Ruffin and a cast of some of New Orleans's best players. Seeing those familiar places reminded me how much fun we had had there, how much of the city's culture I had absorbed, and how good it would be to return.

The morning after we watched the final episodes, we were sitting outside on the rear deck drinking Happy Coffee and taking in the morning sun.

"Did you like the series?" she said.

"I did. It was very surreal. We were just there and to see those places where we spent time was just… well, it took me right back."

"Me too," she said.

"I want to see more," I said. "Maybe we could plan that trip through the south we talked about with Joanie and Jimmy."

"We could do that," she said. "Fly into someplace central and rent a car and end up in New Orleans."

"That would be a great road trip. Start out in Mississippi. You know how I feel about places. I would like to feel the spirit of that area."

"We could see Joanie and Jimmy," she said. "They would put us up for a day or two."

"Play a little music."

"Jimmy knows some good players," she said. "It would be a good trip."

I wasted no time moving my personal items to the Ranch, which timed perfectly with my last days at the grocery store. For the first time in many years, my life felt like I was in control. It was a major shift in my life; I was with someone I felt totally at ease with, a woman I believed honestly loved me. There was no underlying tension about who I was or who Rose was. We had no disagreements or angry moments between us. There was no butting of heads, no fights over what somebody should or should not do, and no conflicts regarding food, drink or ways to have fun.

Rose was an adventurous lover and the Ranch, despite its modest trappings, had its own relaxed personality. It was quiet and removed from the bustle of an otherwise aggressive world. I felt like all the daily pressures of modern life avoided Welcome Road and shadowed other less fortunate places.

The Welcome Road community was a protective group and an interesting cross section of islanders. Rose's closest neighbors were a Boeing executive and an estate facilitator. Adjacent to the Ranch, an Australian native coached youth soccer and ran his upholstery business out of his double garage. A fellow Vietnam vet who did maintenance work for a school district lived across the road from the market and would stop by periodically to see if Rose needed any help with the Ranch. Rose had recently taken a Native American single mother under her wing, helping her develop gluten-free baked goods they sold jointly through the market. A frequent visitor was a young man with dreadlocks who was working on alternative housing and engineering designs with an eye towards self-sufficiency. The parade of interesting people stopping by kept life on the Ranch stimulating.

We had an early spring that year providing us with more sunny days than usual which meant we spent more time outside on the decks. From the barn, Rose brought out two plastic Adirondack-style chairs and a small plastic table that we set up on the front deck which got full sun from noon to dusk.

When I got home from the shop, I would make a margarita for myself and pour Rose a glass of wine with an ice cube and we would sit out on the deck in the late afternoon warmth. We would check in with each other's day and talk about anything that struck our fancy at the moment.

"I was thinking," she said, one afternoon, "what it might be like to be in New Orleans."

"We already talked about a trip to the south."

"No, I mean full time," she said. "I was thinking I could sell the Ranch and you could sell your business and we could move to New Orleans."

"Wow," I said. "That is one big thought, Miss Rose."

"I know," she said, "but wouldn't that be exciting?"

"Exciting yes. Practical…I'm not so sure. What would we do there?"

"I was thinking we would open a bar. A small bar with a place to live above it."

"A bar?" I said. "You and me running a bar."

"I've worked in one. We would have a stage, like the Spotted Cat, and you would have a place to play. And we'd live upstairs."

As Rose ran down all the things we'd offer and the musicians we would attract, I tried to process this new and somewhat unsettling idea.

"So we would just up and move to New Orleans?" I said.

"Start a new life," she said. "Start something fresh…something truly ours."

We didn't immediately come to a definitive decision about a possible move to New Orleans, but we did talk about it more. It was a huge proposition that would take both of us out of what we had each been doing for a long time. I loved New Orleans and I loved that Rose thought enough of us that she saw us in this major undertaking together. That to me was the big takeaway from the whole conversation, but I still gave thought to the idea. My biggest concern was access to a V.A. facility in case my cancer returned. I did a Google search of V.A. hospitals and found there were several in the greater New Orleans area.

A week after our New Orleans conversation, Rose told me a friend of hers was coming up to spend a few days with us. Linda was a one-time traveling companion of Rose's who now taught school in Reno. She had a daughter in Eastern Washington she needed to visit, and there was a chance she and Rose would have to deliver a mattress Rose had been storing for her in the barn.

The day Linda arrived put our New Orleans conversation on hold. When I got home that night, the two of them were already deep into the herb and cocktail hour. Rose tried to bring me up to speed with their reminiscence over the years and it was clear they had spent considerable time on the road together.

Linda was a loud presence and could talk at great length seemingly without taking a breath. All I could do was sit back and listen. I didn't really mind being out of the conversation at this point and totally understood two old friends getting together after being apart for a while. Then the conversation turned from remembering the past to planning the future.

"So my idea is a bunch of small trailers," Rose said. "Weekend getaways for the bohemians across the water."

"Oh I can see that," Linda said. "There's plenty of room out here."

"Five acres, including the chicken area."

"It would take some cleaning up."

"Of course," Rose said. "I have friends with heavy equipment who could come in and grade the area. I've been selling a lot of the wood Bob had milled and that should all be gone soon."

"Maybe five or six trailers around a nice grassy area," Linda said.

"A rustic BnB. Pot friendly with fresh baked goods in the morning."

"I love it," Linda said.

"And you could have your trailer up here, closer to the house."

"Well, not too close," Linda said. "I don't want to be right outside your door."

"Not with all the room we have here," I chimed in.

"So," Linda said, "tell me more about you two."

By ten o'clock I had had enough of the loud talk and curious plans for a trailer park BnB.

"Yeah, I'm a bit road weary," Linda said. "We can continue tomorrow."

Rose made up the new sofa bed for Linda, and we called it a night. Rose and I got into bed, which was only separated from the living room by the half wall with the stuffed game birds on it.

"I'm sorry she's such a talker," Rose whispered.

"She's just happy to see you," I whispered back.

"Non-stop. But it's good to see her. We've had a lot of good times over the years."

"Apparently," I said. "I was exhausted just listening."

"Are you okay with her here?"

"Of course," I said. "She's your friend."

"She's going to help me keep the Ranch."

"You mean permanently?"

"We can talk tomorrow," she whispered. "She's just on the other side."

"So there's no fooling around while she's here?"

"Not necessarily. How quiet can you be?"

The next morning I was the first one up and stepped out onto the rear deck for a smoke. It was a beautiful morning and having Linda asleep on the sofa threw off my morning routine. Bella came to the sliding door looking to be fed, so I slipped back inside and quietly filled her bowl with kibbles.

Linda got up and immediately started talking where she had left off the night before. Rose stumbled into the room and before long the two of them were chattering like two magpies. All I wanted to do was take a shower, get dressed and leave them to their reunion.

Linda stayed with us for another four days and the night before she left, we had a little dinner gathering of a few neighbors and friends. The evening came to an end with everyone being gracious and wishing Linda a safe trip home. The following morning she was on the road, without Rose, to deliver her daughter's new mattress.

I refrained from saying anything right then about "the rustic BnB" idea out of respect for Rose's friendship with Linda. But that night, we were sitting out on the front deck enjoying the last of the sun when I couldn't hold back my thoughts.

"So did you and Linda come to any decision?"

"I explained what was happening with the property and how I might need to buy out Bob's daughter."

"And?"

"She said she had the money whenever I needed it."

"Well that's good, I think."

"We talked about developing the property, and how we could make it more profitable."

"The two of you?"

"Well, she would be a partner."

"A partner."

"For her buy-out money."

"You know partnerships can be tricky," I said.

"I know."

"I've had experience with them. They're like marriages, and most times they turn sour. People change, there's money involved, and then there are legal issues."

"Yes, I'm aware of all that," she said. "I also know I could lose this place if I can't buy out Bob's daughter."

"You have assets," I said. "You told me Bob had equipment that was being sold for the buyout."

"But it hasn't sold."

"Moving someone onto the property and bringing in a bunch of trailers just doesn't seem like…."

"Like what?"

"It doesn't seem like the best long-term answer."

"I can't lose the Ranch," she said. "Where would I go? What would I do?"

"You're not going to lose the Ranch."

"How do you know?"

"You are a widow," I said. "It doesn't matter that Bob didn't change his will. By marriage, you are the rightful owner of the property. No judge is going to throw you off the property and give it to an estranged daughter who hasn't seen her father in years."

"That's easy for you to say. It's not your life on the hook."

"It is if Linda suddenly parks her trailer outside our back door."

"So this is about Linda?"

"I know she's your friend and you have history."

"She has the money that could save the Ranch."

"And she comes with that money. Are you sure you want that kind of relationship with her?"

"I can't lose the Ranch," Rose said.

"Look," I said. "I love you madly. I could be married to you, but I couldn't be married to her too."

"Who said anything about marriage?"

"Think about it," I said. "She moves her trailer here. She's going to be in here first thing in the morning for coffee. You'll spend all day together and of course she'll be invited in for dinner because a good friend wouldn't be left in her trailer with just a can of soup. And she'll be here after dinner and our life will be …well it will no longer be our life."

"It won't be like that. She'll have her own life. We'll just be partners in building the Ranch."

"I thought that's what we would be doing," I said. "Building up the market, expanding the menu. Work Pike Place. Hell what happened to New Orleans?"

"All I know is, I don't want to lose the Ranch. I can't lose it. It's all I have."

Over the next few weeks, there was no further discussion of Linda and her moving to the Ranch. She was still teaching, and she had family issues of her own she was dealing with. It was still unclear if she could afford to retire yet or really wanted to. She saw Rose had someone else in her life now, and I am certain that was on her mind when she left.

For Rose and me, life moved forward. I started to work on her neglected email list of customers, began taking pictures of the dishes she made for her Alzheimer's couple, and thinking of ways to promote the market.

Rose's new batch of chicks was due to arrive any day from a Midwest hatchery, so she spent time getting the empty barn ready for them. She bought two large aluminum cattle tanks, a bale of fresh hay for warm bedding, and new heat lamps for each of the tanks. The chicks would stay in the tubs a few weeks until they were able to fend for themselves in the coop area.

As for us, life moved forward as if nothing had changed.

Chapter Twenty-Nine

"PEOPLE SPEAK HIGHLY OF YOU."

Rose on her own had made arrangements for us to meet with the entertainment coordinator of the Rod 'n Gun Club to see about booking dates for my band. Rose was a born promoter, and the official social director of her Welcome Road tribe. If someone had a birthday, she arranged a party. For special holidays, she would get on the phone and make sure there would be a proper gathering at one of the clubs or at the Ranch. Rose was someone who clearly lived in the moment, as if it were the only moment that mattered.

Some people have a knack for translating enthusiasm into action, and Rose was one of them. It didn't hurt she could be a people-person when she wanted to be, and she could make you feel you were the most important person in the room if she was talking to you. She knew a lot of little things about a wide variety of subjects and if she didn't know anything, she would ask you about it in such a way to make you feel important. And she got along with strong women, because she was strong enough to not feel inferior to them. But beneath her confident exterior there were flashes of vulnerability. On rare occasions, she would take my hand and hold it tight as if testing my acceptance then once I returned her gentle squeeze she would let go as quickly as she had grasped it. No words were spoken; the gesture spoke for itself.

We met the music coordinator in the bar of the club on a Tuesday night, and I told Rose I would let her do the talking. The coordinator joined us at our table, and I ordered us all a drink.

"So," the coordinator said to me, "you're with the band."

"I am," I said, "and we would like to book some dates here."

"They are really good," Rose said. "They've played everywhere on the island and know how to get people up and dancing."

"I've asked around," the woman said, "and people speak highly of you."

"We like everyone to have a good time," I said.

"All my friends love them," Rose said. "They're as good as the groups we've seen here."

"We have a couple of dates available. What do you charge?"

Most of the music venues on the island did not pay for entertainment. The bands either worked for tips or charged a cover. But a private club was different. They brought bands in from Seattle which meant they had to pay and pay well. Whatever the club paid them, I didn't want anything less.

"What did you pay the band last week?" I said.

She gave me a number that was very fair and reflected a respect for the musicians. "That works for us," I said.

"They will pack the house," Rose said.

We agreed on the price and the dates and, with that, our meeting was over and the lady excused herself.

"Congratulations, *El Presidente*," Rose said.

"Thanks to you," I said. I leaned over and kissed her.

"This calls for a celebration," she said. "I'll make some calls and have everybody save the dates. We'll get everybody we know here."

Chapter Thirty

"I'M A SUCKER FOR THE FLAWED."
- ROSE

The warmth of summer arrived early that year. Summer usually didn't officially start in the Northwest until July 5th but, with the arrival of May, hot sunny days were upon us.

Rose ramped up her production of baked goods for the increase in island visitors and developed some new to-go meals for the market. With the new batch of chicks growing big enough to move to the big coops, new things were happening on the Ranch with a look to the future.

The gardens were growing with the early warm days, and I couldn't wait to get back to the Ranch each night and check on my tomatoes and herbs. Sales at the shop had picked up and the band was now playing regularly, but as good as I was feeling, I found it hard to write any new songs. Songwriting had been my salvation when my marriage was falling apart, as a way to express in music what I felt was slipping away. But as soon as the acrimony in my life disappeared, so had my impetus to write music.

I had revisited my interest in making music at the age of fifty. At that time I had been selling books for ten years and, as much as I enjoyed it and it provided me with a living, there was something missing in my life. I felt my most alive when I was creating: developing my seminars on book selling and book collecting, writing book reviews for the Seattle Times, writing two memoirs and a collection of poetry, producing articles for a book collector's magazine and writing my blues opera. They were my most rewarding efforts, but now that I was happy with Rose in my life, the muse was asleep.

We spent our early evenings on the front deck as a leisurely way to unwind from our day's activities. The warm air and stillness enveloped us in the orange glow of the setting sun and was the perfect recipe for easy conversation.

"You should write another opera," Rose said one evening.

“I wish it were that easy,” I said.

“What’s the problem?”

“I had a story to tell,” I said.

“You don’t have another story?”

“Nothing that seems like an opera.”

“But it was so good,” she said. “I liked it a lot.”

“So did I,” I said. “I enjoyed the whole process. Working with the players and writing songs to fit the story, but it was a lot of hard work.”

“So why not another?” she said. “It could have a New Orleans flavor. Maybe a zombie jamboree. Fun music with a lot of great costumes.”

“Something like that needs a story,” I said. “The story is the reason for the opera.”

“So let’s come up with a story,” she said.

I chuckled. “I wish it were that simple. I’ve already got an unfinished memoir trilogy I’m afraid I’ll never complete.”

“What’s the problem?”

“No book three,” I said.

I explained my first two memoirs had been clear in my mind before I wrote them. I had the scenes and the time frames. They both had a natural symmetry: A beginning, a middle and an end, and I knew what the stories were about. But for twenty years, volume three had eluded me. Everything else I considered was nothing more than a series of anecdotal moments that didn't add up to anything of book-length. There was no mystery to solve or conundrum to unravel.

"You're sure there is a volume three?" Rose said.

"I've always felt there would be three."

"And it needs a mystery?"

"Not in the who-dunnit sense," I said. "More of a 'how' or 'why' and what do all the pieces mean?"

"Maybe there's a good reason you don't have number three."

"Like what?" I said.

"Maybe it hasn't happened yet," she said.

I looked at Rose and let her words sink in without comment.

"You can't write a memoir about experiences that haven't happened yet, can you?"

I had always envisioned three volumes and that feeling of three clearly ate at me for twenty years for a reason. I smiled at Rose and shook my head in amusement.

"I hate it when you make so much sense," I said. "It unnerves me."

Rose was a constant source of new awakenings. She had an innate clarity at times that could be completely disarming. Sometimes the best answer to a problem is the simplest. While I wasn't convinced I didn't have a third volume in me, I did back away from my fixation on trying to find it in the life I had already lived. Gone was the friction that had dominated so much of my recent life and I owed that to Rose. Unfortunately, it was friction that had fueled my songwriting.

"So what do you think about another opera?" Rose repeated.

"I'm feeling too happy," I said.

"Who says it can't be happy?"

"It should be serious," I said. "Something more than just some songs and costumes."

"That's where you come in," she said.

"Conflict has driven most of what I've written before," I said. "Darker times."

"Is that what you need?"

"I'd hate to think so," I said, "but for at least a couple dozen songs that's been the case."

"You should be able to write about anything," she said. "Between the two of us, we should be able to find a good story for you to tell.

In the seven years my ex-wife and I lived in our beautiful house on the island, with its big front deck and hot tub over-looking five wooded acres, I couldn't remember ever just relaxing and enjoying the peace and quiet with easy conversation. There was always a disquieting agenda or some ongoing emotional crisis that was more pressing than the idea of just relaxing; and that lack of ease on that property made our life very unpleasant. Between the constant fighting and the financial pressures of the property, I came to hate our house, and our life there paid the price.

The Ranch was completely different. There were tasks to attend to, but once they were done, time was made to sit back and enjoy each other's company.

The evening of our eight-month anniversary, we were sitting on the front deck with the sun beating down hard on us. Hummingbirds darted on and off the feeders while Mr. Kitty stirred up driveway dust giving himself a dirt bath. A Cajun band provided a soulful backdrop through the outside speakers.

"This is the most special place," I said to Rose.

"It *is* nice," she said.

"It's more than nice," I said. "Smell that."

She turned her head to the side to catch what I smelled from the flowers around us. "Lilacs," she said.

"Roses and clematis and honeysuckle," I said. "And it's so still and warm. I don't want to move it's so perfect."

"It *is* perfect," she said. "I never spent enough time out here."

“Reminds me of L.A.,” I said.

“Only the best parts.”

“Away from the city,” I said.

“Up in the hills.”

“Reminds me of Laurel Canyon,” I said, “with the flowers, the quiet, and the music.”

“More like Wonderland Avenue,” Rose said.

“I don’t know Wonderland,” I said. “I do know Laurel Canyon. This makes me think of the canyon a lot.”

“I think of the music on Wonderland and Frank Zappa,” Rose said.

“That’s all we’re missing,” I said.

“We could fix that,” she said. “We have all the room we need. Invite all the neighbors and our friends and you guys can play out here on the deck.”

“Another glass of wine? I asked.

“And a fresh ice cube.”

I returned with our refreshed drinks and sat down in my sun warmed chair.

“Thanks again for your help with the Rod ‘n Gun gigs,” I said

“You guys were great the other night,” she said. “The manager of the club told me it was their biggest night in a long while.”

“But it wouldn’t have happened without you and your table of ten.”

"Sure it would," she said. "It was just a matter of time."

"I mean without your belief. That's important to me."

"You'll be fine," she said. "They loved you guys."

Bella, who had been lounging on the deck between us, suddenly jumped up and began barking, then dashed off the deck and ran at a sprint toward the chicken coops.

Rose jumped up. "Bad birds," she yelled, "bad birds."

Bella ran around the outside of the fenced-in area barking, then suddenly the eagle threatening the girls flew off a low-hanging branch near the coops, circled overhead twice, and flew off to the west. Bella made a cursory pass around the coops then slowly made her way back to us on the deck.

"Good girl," Rose said, "good girl."

Bella sat at attention between us, her eyes searching the sky.

"I do believe somebody deserves a treat," Rose said in a whisper.

I went inside and grabbed two biscuits, and when I returned I gave one to Rose and gave Bella mine. Bella settled back down facing the coop area.

"That was exciting," I said.

"She's so good. I'm so lucky to have her."

"She does work hard," I said. "Nothing gets past her."

"She's worth every nickel I paid for her."

"Can I ask how much?"

"More than eight hundred."

"So she's not a rescue?"

"Not at all, but she was a reject."

"Rejected from what?"

"She has blue eyes. Pure bred Aussies don't, and those are considered the most desirable. She was the last one left in her litter, which is why I got her so cheap."

"She seems so perfect," I said.

"She didn't have to be pure for me to want her," Rose said. "I'm a sucker for the flawed."

Chapter Thirty-One

"It's only kinky the first time."
- Rose

My birthday was on the summer solstice, and Rose treated me to dinner at Gordon's Restaurant overlooking Holmes Harbor. It was a beautiful Sunday night and all the tables were occupied except for the window two-top Rose had reserved for us with a view of Saratoga Passage. We had a nice dinner with Cajun prawns for an appetizer and two filet mignons for the main course.

The evening was subdued, but I enjoyed the company and we had a nice private celebration. I was happy to be with just Rose, having a quiet dinner together without a formal gathering of people.

We ordered the Bananas Fosters Crème Brule dessert to share and two coffees and, after we each took a bite, Rose reached into her purse. She handed me a card with a folded piece of paper inside. I unfolded the paper and there were hand-written lines of what appeared to be a series of notes.

"A poem?" I said.

"Not exactly," she said. "You said you were having a hard time writing a song. I wrote this after we got back from New Orleans. There's a song in there. I thought you could find it."

"Like your tattoo?"

"Something like that."

"This is a first," I said. "No one has ever given me a song for a present…at least not intentionally."

"It seemed appropriate."

"That's why you are the best," I said.

I quickly scanned the lines that on first glance appeared random and disjointed but, there was a thread that seemed to connect them. Numerous references to New Orleans clubs were interspersed with some characters we had encountered there.

"Make it a good song," she said.

"Thank you," I said. "I'll do my best."

When we got back to the Ranch, Bella was waiting for us inside the front door. Rose had saved some of her steak for a Bella treat as she did every time we had dinner out.

I stoked the fire and fed the stove more wood to take the chill out of the house. I gave Bella her late night bone then went into the bedroom and undressed. Rose wasted no time getting undressed and before I knew it she was on top of me.

"Well...happy birthday to me," I said.

Rose took the sash off her robe and loosely tied one end around my left wrist, ran it through the headboard, then loosely tied my right wrist with the other end.

"Oh...we're going down this road?" I said.

"Sssh," she said. "Don't say a word."

She slipped off her robe and leaned forward so her breasts gently touched my face. I reached up to touch her, but she quickly pushed my hand away.

"Don't move," she said." and I don't want you to talk."

She opened my legs and slowly touched her lips to my skin and caressed me with her lips and tongue. When she rose up, her long brown hair draped forward covering her face and I just closed my eyes. She slowly rocked back and forth so our bodies touched, but she held me at bay. She took me in her hand and gently rubbed me against her bare skin, first up and down then from side to side, until she let out a series of deep gasps. She sat straight up until she caught her breath.

"You are going to kill me," she whispered.

I tried to pull her to me, but she slapped me lightly. She stared down at me intensely and, when I tried to kiss her, she slapped me again, this time a little harder. I wasn't sure where the slap was going, but it just made me want to touch her even more. I tried again to kiss her, and she pushed me down. Then she took me in her hand, slowly slipped me inside her and, with a slow grinding motion, she moved me deep inside her again and again until we both finished and she finally collapsed onto me.

"You are really trying to kill me," she said, as she tried to catch her breath.

"I thought you were going to punch me out," I said.

"It's your birthday," she said. "I wanted us to have something special."

"Well…that was something special," I said. "It was starting to feel a little kinky."

"It's only kinky the first time," she said. "Happy birthday, *El Presidente*."

"Don't think I'll forget this one," I said.

"I don't want you to forget," she said. "I want you to remember everything."

Chapter Thirty-Two

"I WANT TO KNOW IT ALL MEANT SOMETHING."
- ROSE

For almost a year, I had been working on turning my book-collecting seminar into a book. It was taking forever to get through the editing process and, with my book designer out of town for a few weeks, publication was now being pushed back to the fall. I wanted to have copies available in time for the Seattle Book Fair in October and at the rate we were going it was going to be close. At our last meeting with Denis, he had presented three cover designs and the most modernistic of the three was the unanimous choice. At dinner that night, I asked Rose if she would work this year's book fair with me and help with selling my book. She left open the possibility, then offered her assessment of another issue.

"I finally finished your books," Rose said.

"I had almost forgotten I had given you copies."

"I'm a deliberate reader," she said.

"And..?"

"They're good," she said.

"Thank you."

"You didn't get to it, though," she said.

"Get to what?"

"They're good, but you missed it."

"I'm not sure what 'it' is," I said. "I did my best to tell the stories I knew." I didn't take her surprise comments on my books so much as a personal attack as a curious commentary that left me wondering what 'it' really was I had supposedly missed.

Both memoirs are coming-of-age stories: *In Different Times* is set in my hometown of Bremerton during the summer of 1966. I was eighteen years old, and my life was turned upside down with the threat of being drafted and sent to Vietnam. I had also experienced and squandered my first significant romance. The second book, *Hundred Waters*, is set in Panama after I enlisted to avoid being drafted into the infantry. It was in Panama where I experienced a different personal awakening; the affection of a woman and the sacrifice she would make for me. I thought about Rose's comment and tried to remember the books and the stories I recounted. For the life of me, I couldn't recall anything I had left unsaid or failed to address. But her comment left me wondering what exactly she thought was missing.

That June was the most beautiful launch of summer we had experienced in recent memory. The days were full of sun and very hot and as a result our vegetable gardens flourished. Every morning I would give everything a good watering before the day's heat hit the plants. Little green tomatoes were popping out everywhere as were the peppers and the slugs. I staked up the taller tomato plants whose load of produce was getting heavier, and I sunk empty plastic containers in the soil then filled them with cheap beer to drown the thirsty slugs.

In the evening when I returned from the shop, I immediately watered everything again and emptied the dead slugs and refilled the containers. Rose told me if I trimmed off the non-producing tomato stalks, more nutrients would go to the producers, so I began trimming my way through twelve huge tomato plants. I took the clippings to the coops where the chickens turned them into food so nothing from the garden was wasted.

The whole routine of tending to my tomatoes was a relaxing way to start and end my days. I had planted them, gave them water and pruned the extraneous branches to give the plants every opportunity to flourish. Tending to them also gave me quiet time to sort out my day and relax. I had also taken charge of the plants around the Ranch and the market and felt responsible for ensuring they stayed alive and blossomed. Just as I was finishing my watering one night, Rose came out with drinks for us and we sat on the front steps just as the sun was setting.

"I talked to Linda today," she said.

"So what's new with her?"

"She's changed her mind about the money. She's not coming to the Ranch."

I looked at Rose and I could see she was upset by the news.

"Maybe it's for the best," I said. "Sometimes things happen for a reason. I'm sure Bob's equipment will sell, and you'll get the money you need."

She looked at me like I had called her a dirty name. "I'm going to check on the chicks," she said and headed off to the barn.

Rose spent a good part of her day tending to her new chicks that were getting bigger and hungrier, but were still susceptible to disease. She had already lost three chicks, which was not out of the norm she said, but she wanted to prevent as many losses as possible which meant checking on them regularly. As if tending to the new chicks, baking and cooking meals for the market didn't make for a full day, one evening while trimming my tomato plants she told me she had started a writing project. She worked on it during the day and would put away her writing pad when I got home.

I moved my trimming operation onto the front deck where the tomato stalks were drooping with fruit that was starting to turn red.

"So tell me about this writing project," I said.

"It's just some things," she said.

"Menus…ideas for the Ranch?"

"Personal things."

"Things you can talk about?"

"It's too early. I'm just writing down things I remember."

"What brought this on?"

"There are things I don't want to forget," she said.

"Is everything okay?"

"I'm not getting younger," she said.

"So, like a memoir?"

"Could be. I have a lot of experiences I'd like to write about. People, places, things that happened. I think it would make a good movie."

"So, now it's a movie," I said. "That's a big leap."

"I'm just remembering a lot of things," she said, "and I don't want them to be lost with me."

"Like what?"

"I'm not sure."

"You must have some idea. Why else the desire to write them down?"

"It feels like the time to do this."

"Has something happened?"

"Now just feels like the time. Before I forget. Besides, there are people here on the island who know film."

"There are," I said, "but writing a book and making a film are two different things. A film can take forever to get made…if ever."

"But I have great stories."

"I bet you do," I said. "Let me know if I can be of help."

"I'm just writing things down now. It's been fun remembering."

"Remembering is good," I said.

"And there is so much to remember. It wears me out just remembering."

I stopped pruning and sat down with my drink. The sun was warm on my face and the margarita tasted sweet and refreshing.

"How did you write your books?" she said.

"The first one took the longest," I said. "Ten years to be exact."

"Ten years," she said. "What took so long?"

"I was learning along the way," I said, "...draft after draft. The second book was the hardest. I couldn't figure out how to tell the story I wanted to tell."

"But obviously you figured it out."

"Eventually. But it took time."

"What was the problem?" she said.

"The second book was not going to be a straight forward narrative," I said. "I read two books; one was Ken Kesey's *Sometimes a Great Notion.* Kesey used multiple voices to tell that story. The other book was by a former CIA pilot and he used telegrams, letters and official documents to tell his story. Those two approaches showed me how I could tell the *Hundred Waters* story."

"But the reasons," she said. "Why those stories?"

I thought about her question for a moment and tried to recall the "why" of those stories. In both cases, images and scenes were crystal clear and had stayed with me over the years. Especially the ending. I knew how the stories ended; what I needed to uncover was how I got to the end. What were the events that led to the final scenes? What was the story in the scenes that led to the ending? The longer the images stayed with me, the more I saw them as leading toward something bigger than the individual parts.

"They were like stones in my shoe," I said. "They kept rubbing at me and they wouldn't go away." There was something unknown about each book, I told her, something I needed to find out. It was like an answer resided in the various images and scenes, and it was up to me to connect them. I had to write the story to find the answer," I said, "if that makes sense."

"It does, but you didn't get it."

"Maybe *you* didn't get it," I said.

"Maybe you held back," she said.

"Maybe it meant something you missed," I said. "Something bigger than the individual parts. That 'something' that won't let you forget and makes you remember until you write it out. Maybe that's the it."

"But in each case," she said, "you were remembering."

"Not just remembering to remember," I said. "What I was remembering were the pieces of a puzzle I believed held something bigger. A story of something larger than the individual pieces. There are things that happened, scenes I felt held a story if they were accurately remembered."

"And that's the reason you wrote those stories?" she said.

"The things I remembered happened for a reason," I said, "and they wouldn't go away. I had to write them so I could let go of them and move on."

"But how did you know they were books?"

Whenever someone asked what my books were about, I couldn't begin to tell them. The stories were about a lot of things. All I could say was "It's a long story" because it was a long story. In fact, each book was a long story of a lot of smaller stories.

"When I couldn't describe the story in a sentence," I said. "Then I knew I needed to write them out to know what they all meant."

"That's what I want," Rose said. She stared off toward the chicken coops. "I want to know my life has meant something."

"I'm not sure writing a book will give you that," I said.

Chapter Thirty-Three

"IT'S THE UNEXPECTED THAT CHANGES OUR LIVES."

Sunday July 10th marked the ten-month anniversary of our first meeting, and I was feeling on top of the world. It was also the day Marian was having an early birthday gathering of close friends at the Bloom's Winery Tasting Room at Bayview Corner. That morning I got up like any other morning, made myself a cup of Happy Coffee and eased into the day by walking up to the market and giving the plants a good watering. I opened the market and made note of what baked goods Rose would need to replace then slowly made my way back to the house. I checked on my tomato and pepper plants before I went inside where Rose was brewing up her coffee. I gave her a morning kiss and took a seat at the kitchen table. Rose sat down and was unusually quiet.

"Feeling okay?" I asked.

"I'm fine," she said.

"If you're not feeling well, Marian would understand if we didn't make her party."

"No," she said, "I'm good."

"Today is the tenth," I said.

"Okay," she said, quizzically.

"That makes ten months we have been together."

She didn't say anything which made me think she wasn't feeling well. "Are you sure you're okay?"

"Yes."

"How are we doing then?"

She looked down at her coffee and I could feel something wasn't right. She reached for a cigarette. "There is no we," she said.

"Of course there is. Look at us."

"I don't want to live together," she said.

"Excuse me."

"I don't want a boyfriend. I don't want to live with anyone. I want to live alone."

I was so stunned at the words coming from her mouth I couldn't speak; they were the antithesis of what I expected to hear on our anniversary. I looked at her, waiting for the words to sink in so I could respond, but I was speechless. Time stopped, and then I felt the words tear through me like a sharp knife, and when I looked at Rose I just saw her sad eyes looking back at me.

"I can't believe what I'm hearing," I said.

"It's not about you," she said. "It's all about me."

"It is about me. You are breaking my heart. So that makes it about me. About us."

"There is no us," she said. "I don't want to be responsible for anyone else."

Again her words cut deep into me and the pain they inflicted tore through my insides. I was there physically but something much deeper inside me had vanished…washed away with her words. I felt too small for the kitchen table, and my body began to shake.

"I don't want you to be responsible for me," I said. "Where is this coming from?"

"It's nothing you did," she said.

"I thought we were good. The last time I checked in with you, you said we were good."

"What do you want me to say?"

"I want you to tell me what's happened," I said. "Where this is coming from."

She didn't respond. She just stared down at her coffee.

"We haven't fought. No arguments. None of the things that tear people apart."

"Do you want to fight?" she said.

"Fuck no!" I said. "I want to know why you're doing this…from out of nowhere?"

"I just don't want to be with anyone."

"Just like that," I said. "One day we're all fine, making plans, and the next day you want to be alone. It makes no sense."

"Probably not," she said. "But for what it's worth, there's nobody else."

"It still doesn't answer my question. Why?"

"Look," she said, "we're not having a family, we're not building a life together…."

"What couple in their sixties builds a family?"

"We don't have a future."

"No future. What about our talk of New Orleans? The trip to the south? The plans we had for the Ranch and building up the market? That all sounded like a future to me."

"Look," she said, "I just don't want to be with anyone. There are things I need to do. I don't know what else to say. I just want what I want right now."

"Right now?"

"I've done all I can. My work is done. I'm sorry if it hurts you."

"Hurts me? I've loved you since I first met you. Now…out of nowhere… you tell me we're through. It's beyond hurt. You have broken my heart."

She just stared down at her cigarette, the smoke trailing up in a straight line between us. Clearly something had shifted, but for the life of me I had no warning of something so drastic. I tried to remember anything I might have said or done that could have caused such a radical change in our relationship, but there was nothing I could recall.

"I just want to be alone," she said. "I'm bisexual and I have things to do."

"I don't care about your other proclivities," I said. "We have been so good together. The best lover of my life, and someone I'm most comfortable with."

"Well…sex complicates things," she said.

I looked at her with complete disbelief. It was like I had been living in an alternate universe of joy and affection for the last ten months and then I was suddenly dropped back onto a hostile and unrecognizable Earth.

"And besides," she said, "familiarity breeds contempt."

"So what's my level of contempt right now?" I asked.

"Zero," she said. "I'm just saying it can lead to that."

"It doesn't have to."

"But it usually does," she said.

"That's bullshit. Not if two people truly care about each other."

"You're divorced."

"And you're a widow," I said.

"You left your wife."

"Yes I did and your husband died."

"Leaving someone is different than having them die."

"I gave my marriage every chance to get better."

"Leaving was a choice."

"A painful choice, but staying together would have been more damaging."

"But you did leave."

"I did but I'm not sorry, because I never would have met you."

"I've done all I can. The cards have spoken. I have things I want to get to. I want to write my life while I can."

"The cards? And you can't write with me in your life?"

"I need to focus, and I can't do that now. I need you to find a place to live by September."

It was clear from her responses we were not involved in a negotiation. This was not an issue of someone's bad behavior, a nasty habit or an indiscretion…all of which could be addressed. Something else had shifted and shifted dramatically with apparently no wiggle room or, for me, any reasonable explanation.

I went outside and sat on the front deck alone. The sun had lost its yellow brightness. The tall pine trees around me were like a wall blocking out the horizon, and the roses had lost their sweet aroma. Where life had been so peaceful the day before, suddenly thunder clouds darkened everything. The person who had brought so much joy into my life in so many ways had just ripped out my heart. Everything about the Ranch felt far away…alien and unfamiliar. The pain of loss was immediately replaced by my need to move.

I drove into town and tried to work but my heart wasn't into it. All I could think about was what went wrong and where was I going to find a place to live as soon as possible. I immediately contacted a few close friends and told them I was looking for an apartment. At 5 pm I gave serious consideration whether to go to Marian's birthday party given the sudden change in Rose and my relationship. The longer I weighed whether to go or not, the more I realized I didn't want to avoid wishing Marian well on her special day.

I closed the shop and made the short drive to Bayview and found Marian at a table with the owners of the winery. I greeted her with a hug and wished her a happy birthday.

"Thanks for coming," she said. "Where's Rose?"

"I'm sure she's on her way," I said.

"Is everything okay?" she asked. "You don't look well."

"Rose and I aren't together anymore."

"You're what?"

"She broke it off this morning," I said.

"I don't believe it," she said. "What happened?"

"I have no idea. She just said she didn't want to be together any more, and she didn't want to be responsible for anyone."

"I'm shocked," Marian said. "I thought everything was so perfect with you guys."

"So did I…until this morning."

"Just out of the blue she said that?"

"I thought everything was fine," I said. "We were happy. She took me out to dinner on my birthday. Then this on our anniversary. I have no idea where this is coming from."

"I'm just shocked," Marian said. "You two seemed so perfect for each other. I had no idea."

Marian embraced me, and we held each other tight.

"I don't want to put a damper on your party," I said. "I don't think I can stay under the circumstances. I didn't want to just not show up, but I should leave before Rose gets here."

"I'm so sorry to hear this," she said.

"Yeah, me too."

With that, I headed back to my car just as Rose pulled into the parking lot. We looked at each other and, without any words, I got in my car and drove back to Langley. I went to Prima and sat at the bar and tried to make sense out of what had happened to completely change my life for the worse. I drank until nine then drove back to the Ranch. Rose was sitting in her chair when I came in, and she quickly put away her writing pad.

"Hey," she said.

"Don't stop on my account," I said.

"That's okay. I was done."

I made a drink and went outside onto the rear deck and watched the last slivers of the sunset. Rose came out and sat down at the table.

"You left Marian's party just as I got there," Rose said.

"It felt wrong to be there when she was trying to celebrate her special day."

"I had planned on telling her about us, but you had already told her."

"I couldn't lie when she asked how I was."

We both sat there without talking, just taking in the last of the day's golden light.

"Any business today?" she asked.

"You don't have to make small talk with me," I said.

"Please don't hate me," she said.

"Hate you?" I said. "How could I hate you? I've done nothing but love you."

She sat back in her chair and sipped her wine. "The coyotes were through here today," she said.

"That right?"

"Bella was right on them."

"I bet she was."

"She ran them off and stood guard until they were gone. They're looking for water."

I didn't say anything.

"I had a good day at the market," she said. "Sold out of muffins and to-go dinners."

We sat there in the day's fading warmth, and it was hard for me to engage in the easy-going conversation we had once enjoyed. I just looked at her and couldn't believe this was the same woman who the day before had made me the happiest man in the world.

"I'm going to water the plants," I said. "I'll sleep on the sofa bed."

I went out front and gave everything a good watering which took a good hour, but I was in no hurry to go inside. By ten-thirty, I figured Rose would be in bed and we wouldn't have to go through all the awkwardness of being in the same room together. There were no more plans to discuss, no loving interest in anyone's day or things that might concern the future. An emptiness fell over the Ranch, and I was an outsider in what had become my home. There was no need to talk because as she said, "there is no us." I was now just a guest temporarily staying under her roof.

When I finished watering, I went inside and pulled out the sofa bed. Rose immediately came out of the bedroom.

"Don't sleep out here," she said.

"I think it's best."

"Come and sleep in the bed."

"You can't be serious," I said.

"I'm asking you to sleep in the bed. It's ridiculous for you to sleep out here."

"Seems normal to me," I said, "under the circumstances."

"It's not," she said. "You're being stubborn."

"How is that going to affect my contempt factor?"

"Please," she said. "Don't sleep out here. Bella wants you in the bed."

"That's not good enough."

"I don't want you sleeping out here."

"What you want doesn't make me feel any better."

For the next week we both went about our regular routines as though nothing had changed even though everything had. I still got up first and walked up to the market and gave all the plants a good watering; then I opened the market and made a list of what had sold. I watered the tomatoes and the plants around the house before I went into the shop.

Ten days into our separation, Rose fell off the rear deck and hurt her right wrist. She hurt it bad enough that she couldn't use it for the simplest tasks around the house.

"How did it happen?" I asked when I got home.

"I was watering the hanging basket there," she said, "and next thing I know I'm on the ground."

"Did you blackout?"

"I just fell," she said. "It's not a big deal. But I can't use my right hand."

With Rose unable to lift or hold anything with her right hand, her ability to bake and cook and tend the chickens was greatly impacted. So in the morning I would water the hanging baskets and help with anything she needed done in the kitchen. I made up muffin and brownie batter and did any chopping she needed for her to-go meals. I carried the daily fifty-pound bag of chicken food down to the coops, fed the birds, and refilled their water cans. Then I went to the shop for the day.

It was good I was still staying at the Ranch when Rose hurt her wrist, because she couldn't drive with just one good hand. Once a week I drove her to the mainland to shop at food wholesalers and up the island to buy chicken feed. I felt good being able to help her when she needed someone the most. She had neighbors who could have come by periodically, but there were a lot of little things she needed help with that wouldn't wait until after work. I also now had a reason for being at the Ranch. If I had immediately found another place to live, I would probably never have heard about her fall, but I was there and I was happy to help.

My "drop-dead" date to leave the Ranch was September 15th. And on the tenth I found a small place to rent not far out of town. I gave Rose the news, and started moving my things out immediately. I boxed up my possessions that were not necessities on a daily basis and began dropping them off in my storage locker on my way to the shop each morning.

By the morning of the 15th, all I had left at the Ranch were some clothes. I did my usual set of morning tasks one last time. I watered the plants around the market then opened it for the day. My tomatoes were getting big and deep red, and I was about to leave them after one more good watering. Not being able to see my tomatoes and peppers ripen made me sad considering all the time I had spent tending them.

I loaded four bags of chicken food into my car and drove them down to the coops and stacked them outside the gate. I fed the birds, filled their water cans and then closed the gate behind me one last time.

As I was returning to the house, I saw Rose walk from the house into the barn. I was sure she wanted to avoid any more uncomfortable conversations between us. I brought out the last of my clothes that were hanging in the armoire and draped them over the layer of boxes in my trunk. I made one last trip through the house looking for anything of mine I might have missed. Rose was standing at the rear of my car when I came out, her right hand wrapped in her brace. She was leaning against the rear hatch of the car staring down at the ground. When she looked up her eyes were swollen and red and there were moisture streaks on her cheeks, cutting through the dust she had stirred up in the barn.

"Are you alright?" I asked.

"I'm fine," she said.

"Is there anything else I can do for you before I go?"

"No," she said, "I'll manage."

"Are you sure? I have time."

"I'll be fine."

"I put extra bags of feed down at the coops, and everything has been watered for the morning."

"Thank you," she said. "Rozie and Marian will be by after work."

We just stood by the car for a minute without saying anything. The time for talking was officially over with little left to say. Rose had already said everything.

"It's been nice having you here the last two months," she said.

"It's not how I saw our lives unfolding," I said. "I didn't see this coming at all."

"Believe me," she said. "It's not about you. Honestly."

"I love you," I said, "and you have broken my heart."

"I'll always love you, *El Presidente*," she said.

"You've taken away the sweetest thing in my life."

"It's not easy for me," she said.

"I hope your life will be better now without me in it," I said.

"I watched you put your clothes in the car and… and…all I could do was cry. That's why I couldn't be in the house."

"This is what you want," I said. "It doesn't change how much I love you or how much I want you in my life, but it's clearly what you want."

"I can't see you for a couple of months," she said. "I just can't. Please don't hate me."

"I wish I could hate you," I said. "I might feel better, but I can't. I just can't."

I got in my car, started it up, and slowly drove out Welcome Road, passed the market and finally off the Ranch, leaving Rose and Bella in my rear view mirror.

Chapter Thirty-Four

"I think she was just afraid."
- Rozie

September 15, 2015 marked the end of the most wonderful period in my life. Exactly one year after I met Rose, our life together ended. The days that followed were the emptiest I have known. I was sixty-eight, and my life with a loving woman felt over. I had no desire to see anyone or go anywhere public; if I could have willed total disappearance, I would have. All the things that had been said and done over the last year replayed in my head like an endless loop of painful reminders of what had once been the joys of my life: The good and loving things alongside the hurtful words that ended my year with Rose. I tried desperately to bring order out of the confusion which only led to more and more questions I had no answers for. I tried to find a thread to follow in hopes of unraveling what had happened to us so suddenly. For several weeks, I searched my memory for answers by reliving our time together hoping to uncover a clue to what had changed, and all I got was more confusion. I was so frustrated all I could think about was getting away and moving to some other place, a place with no connection to Rose. But the thought of moving my business and giving up my bandmates kept me from just driving off the island toward anywhere else.

I had been gone from the Ranch three weeks when one Sunday morning I ran into Rose's neighbors Rozie and Kennedy outside the restaurant next to my shop. They asked how I was doing and shared how sorry and confused they were over what had happened.

"It doesn't make sense," Rozie said. "I thought you guys were perfect together."

"I thought so too," I said.

"I think she was just afraid," Rozie said.

"Afraid? Did she say that?"

"No. That's just my feeling."

"Afraid of what?"

"Like I said, it's just my feeling."

There was a pause between us and Rozie looked over at Kennedy and without saying anything there was clearly a question in their looks at each other.

"I think we should," Rozie whispered to Kennedy.

"I'm not so sure," Kennedy said.

"Rose didn't want us to say anything," Rozie finally said, "but I think you should know."

"What?"

"She's in the hospital."

"Oh shit," I said. "Is it her heart?"

"No," Rozie said. "She had a cancerous tumor removed from her bladder."

"How is she? Is she alright?"

"They got it," Kennedy said, "and she's recovering."

"That's good," I said.

They told me she was at Providence Hospital in Everett, a short ferry ride away, and she was doing fine.

"And she didn't want me to know?" I said.

"That's what she said," Rozie said. "But when I saw you, I just felt you should know."

"I appreciate that. She still means the world to me."

"I know," Rozie said. They had errands to run so we said our goodbyes, and I thanked them for telling me about Rose's situation. I went back to the shop, thought about Rose in the hospital, and I immediately closed the shop and drove for the ferry.

I got to the hospital forty-five minutes later. I asked the guard at the information desk for Rose's room number. I was told there was no one admitted with the name I gave him. I tried the two other names I heard friends refer to her by and Brena Gustafson got me a room number.

I found Rose's room on the fourth floor recovery area. Marian was there and they were watching the Seahawks game.

"Hey you," Rose said, when I knocked on the open door.

I walked over and bent down and kissed her lightly on the lips. "Aren't you a sight," I said.

"I'm sure I am."

"How are you doing?" I asked.

"Much better," she said. "They took a tumor the size of a baseball out of me."

"And now?"

"I feel good," she said.

"You look good," I said.

"I'm sure I'm a mess," she said.

"You look beautiful," I said. Marian smiled and excused herself. I leaned into Rose and looked into her eyes. "Rozie told me you were here. She said you told her not to tell me. Did you think I wouldn't want to know?"

"I'll talk to her," Rose said.

"That's not necessary," I said. I took her hand and smiled down at her. "This is not the way I ever wanted to see you."

"Don't get all mushy now," she said. The sharp tone in her voice took me by surprise and I could feel my presence was for some reason an intrusion. Marian came back into the room, and I stepped away from Rose.

"I was concerned when Rozie told me you had surgery," I said. "I just couldn't stay away."

"I'm doing fine," Rose said.

"So how long had this been going on?" I asked.

"The doctors said it's probably been inside me for months."

"You had the tumor for months?"

"But they got it all, they say. And Marian is taking good care of me."

I looked over at Marian and smiled. Suddenly the air felt heavy with awkwardness and I felt out of place. It was as though I had crashed a private party, and I knew I couldn't stay.

"I can see this was not a good idea," I said. "I'm happy you're okay and doing well. I should get back to the island."

"Thanks for coming by," Rose said.

"Be well," I said, and I gave Marian a goodbye hug on my way out.

Visiting Rose in the hospital that day was the most uncomfortable feeling I had ever had with her. She couldn't have been colder. If nothing else, it convinced me there was no going back and Rose made that perfectly clear. The only problem was moving forward. There was too much that still felt unfinished.

Chapter Thirty-Five

"For the light to shine brightly,
the darkness must be present."
- Francis Bacon

Fall eased into the winter months of rain and darkness, and I was learning to be alone. As so many times in the past, I turned to music as my way of shedding light on the dark places in my life. I tried to give voice to my concerns about Rose and her cold treatment of me at the hospital. I kept coming back to things Rose had said like "It's all about me," and "I'll always love you," and "you make me feel beautiful" and the words would spin around inside me until I got them down on paper.

I turned questions into lyrics followed by more questions and possible answers. The more I wrote, the deeper I dug for reasons, but again answers were hard to come by. I had more questions than either of us had answers for. But underneath the confusion, my affection for Rose had not diminished. I was lost in disbelief and adrift without Rose, but I had not lost my concern or love for her. She had sparked a new sense of life in me that had been missing for a long time. It was hard to assess exactly what had transpired between us, but I knew it was something real, tangible, and not yet over.

As weeks turned into months, Rose's absence in my life left a gaping hole in my chest. It was an emptiness that no amount of alcohol or busy work could fill.

Rose in many ways was a very private person. She had a Facebook page but never posted anything of a personal nature on it. I, on the other hand, did use my personal and music pages for band announcements or book-related subjects. The very first time she spent the night at my apartment, I made us breakfast before she went home in the morning. While she showered, I set two places on my dining table with two empty plates and steaming cups of coffee. I was so happy to have her in my life that morning, I wanted my friends to know something good was happening for me. There were no names or faces in the posting, just a photo of the dining table and two place settings. After I took the picture, I captioned it "Breakfast for two" when I uploaded it. It was just our little secret with a hint of mystery. Shortly after I left the Ranch, she unfriended me on Facebook which hurt as much as her cold reception at the hospital.

There had always been opportunities for conversation between Rose and me and more times than not those exchanges resulted in something interesting unfolding. During one of our casual conversations early in our relationship, she had mentioned, almost in passing, that she had been abandoned by her mother at an early age. She said it so matter-of-factly you would have thought she was just commenting on the day's weather. The more I thought about that admission and the fact she had done the same thing with her own daughter, the more Rose's early life came into focus.

Being abandoned by a mother is a serious act of rejection, and I couldn't imagine the damage that decision had on Rose's sense of value and worth as a human being. And then she repeated the same act with a child of her own.

Hearing that her mother walked away from her as a child made me think of when my mother was diagnosed with multiple sclerosis when I was five; from then on I was the part-time caretaker of the woman who gave me life. Her role in my life went from mother to a loved one I nursed; the woman I cooked for, helped in and out of the bathroom and picked up after. Although she lived another forty years, I lost my mother the year she was diagnosed and never got her back. Even though she was still in my life and I loved her, nothing was ever the same once the disease took over her life. And I couldn't wait to leave home and my role as caretaker, and to find my own life. From that point on, I purposely avoided situations where I had no control over my life.

On another occasion, Rose told me she had found a previous lover, a musician, dead on their living room couch from an overdose. I told her I had also found a good friend dead in his bathroom and had the painful responsibility to inform his parents. Finding the lifeless body of a friend or loved one leaves an indelible wound on you making it hard to get that close to anyone else. These were not the results of scripted speeches or inordinate prying but extemporaneous statements of fact, like so many pieces of a puzzle dropped into our conversation. Those shared episodes of personal loss were telling moments I was glad we had shared with each other; they were insightful glimpses into darker places.

The holidays that year after our separation came and went with no contact between us. I sent Rose a Christmas card with a personal note inside, but I never received a reply. On New Year's Eve we crossed paths at the pub across from my one-time apartment on 2nd Street. Rose was out celebrating with Mike and Marian. When Marian saw me she hesitantly approached me with a hug and a strange feeling of awkwardness. Rose remained by the front door of the pub and just looked at me, but neither of us approached the other. Finally I just left the festivities and walked past her at the front door without saying a word. In January, I sent her a "Happy 65th" birthday card with another personal note apologizing for being rude as I exited the pub on New Years. Again I received no response.

The night of Rose's birthday, I was sitting at the bar of the Village Pizzeria watching a football game when I saw Marian and Mike enter carrying a bunch of balloons and wrapped packages. I quickly realized what the occasion was. I had chosen the wrong place to have a drink.

"Hey you," Marian said embracing me. "What are you up to?"

"Just having a drink," I said, "and watching the game. I don't have to guess what you're doing tonight."

"Just a little birthday celebration."

"Well, give her my best," I said.

The restaurant staff pushed together three tables behind me and slowly Rose's friends began arriving and taking up seats around the tables. One of Rose's Welcome Road neighbors Victoria, a warm-hearted woman I knew only briefly, saw me and excitedly asked if I would be joining them.

"No," I said. "I didn't get the invite."

Rose eventually arrived and took her place at the assembled tables. The gathering of friends was full of laughter and shared stories. I had become the invisible man; he who must not be acknowledged. That was a painful pill to swallow. I thought to myself: "So much for 'I can't see you for a couple of months.'" There was no seeing me at all. The festivities finally took their toll on me; I immediately paid my check and left before the game was over.

I spent the next six months playing as much music as I could book. I was writing songs left and right, some of which didn't pan out but others did. There were many references to New Orleans in those songs and some special moments Rose and I had shared.

In May of 2016, I booked two nights in a recording studio on the island to cut twelve new songs I had written. Part of the reason to record was to capture the current band lineup which was really good and tight and another was I hoped Rose would hear what I had written with her in mind. She no longer came to any of our appearances and the CD was clearly going to be my tribute to her. I titled it "Welcome Road" after the song by the same name that spoke to who Rose was and that I was no longer welcome where she lived. But the one song I really wanted her to hear was "The Rose of Bourbon Street." I wrote it as a lament at first for the special woman I had lost. I based it on the photograph I took of her in New Orleans standing in the middle of Bourbon Street looking beautiful. She had told me it was her favorite picture of herself, and it always reminds me of how much fun we had in that great city. We also recorded "Lost Lover's Lounge," which I wrote based on the "notes" she gave me for my birthday.

I scheduled the release of the CD for our August appearance during the Bayview Summer Street Dance series, the same outdoor event where Rose and I first met two years earlier, almost to the day.

The night of the dance was a beautiful August evening and a large crowd came out to dance and socialize. We were halfway through our first set when I saw Rose walking through the crowd with her neighbor Victoria. I was both surprised and happy to see her, but I didn't know what to expect. Would she avoid me, would we talk?

We finished our first set and I made another announcement we were launching our first CD and they were available next to the stage area. I saw Rose walk over to the sale table and buy a copy and talk with a mutual friend. I decided to get a beer and stretch my legs.

Twenty minutes later, we roared into our second set and I quickly noticed Rose and Victoria were now seated in the folding chair section, four rows behind the dance area. They were in clear view of the band, and I could see Rose had a new grey streak on the left side of her long brown hair. As I sang, I couldn't take my eyes off her. It was as though no one else was there. She listened and watched us, and I kept my eyes on her hoping I might see a sign from her that might signal any kind of change toward me.

The evening was winding down to the last few songs when Rose and Victoria suddenly got up and slowly made their way behind the dancers toward the nearby parking lot. I watched them as they crossed laterally in front of us hoping to see something positive: A wave, a smile, anything. Just as they reached the edge of the dance area Rose paused, looked back at me, smiled and continued to look at me until I acknowledged her with a nod, then she disappeared into the parking area. The 'look back' and her smile were small but hopeful signs that night. I wasn't sure if they meant anything significant in the big scheme of things, but they did give me hope we might see each other again.

Two weeks after our street dance performance, the first fall indoor dance took place in Bayview Hall adjacent to the area where we had played the final outdoor dance. It was Wednesday evening, August 31, 2016. I arrived early and saw members of the band gathered near the rear of the building and I joined them before they started playing.

I listened to the first five songs, but the volume of the band and the hard surfaces of the hall made it hard to listen inside the building. I stepped out the side door and decided to walk across the parking lot to the Taproom for a quick drink. I chatted with a few friends and, when I finished my drink, I headed back across the parking lot to listen to more music. I saw a group of people outside the front door and immediately recognized Marian. Rose was standing next to her, leaning against the railing wearing her signature blue bandana. They clearly saw me, which made it hard for me to avoid the front entrance. I walked up the ramp to the porch and Rose immediately came up and embraced me.

"Hey," Rose said.

"Hey to you," I said hesitantly.

"Joanie's in the hospital."

Her announcement caught me off guard. "Joanie who?" I said.

"Joanie…of Joanie and Jimmy. You met them in New Orleans."

"Oh sure," I said. "What's the problem?"

"Lung issues. She's not doing well."

"I'm sorry to hear that," I said. "How serious?"

"I'm not sure," she said. "I'm waiting to hear more. But I thought you would like to know."

"Thanks," I said. "I hope she's okay."

"I'll know more later."

The situation was awkward, and I had no idea what to say once Rose and I were face to face. The puzzled expression on Marian's face indicated she wasn't sure what would unfold, and an odd tension fell over the porch. Marian stood quietly, looking at us. Neither Rose nor I said anything. The music blared loud through the open front door and I was about to excuse myself when Rose took my arm and led me off the porch.

"I have to put this in the car," she said, holding up a small paper bag.

Her Jeep was parked right next to the ramp in the handicapped space and, as I came around the car, I saw Bella in the front seat.

"Hey Bella girl," I said. I stuck my hand through the half-opened window and softly stroked her head. She repeatedly nuzzled her nose against my hand and tried to get her head out the half open window. Rose dropped off her bag and closed the door.

"You stay here," she told Bella.

Rose slowly led me into the darkest part of the parking lot.

"You look like you've lost weight," she said, as we walked.

"You look good yourself. How's the arm?"

"Turns out I had broken it."

"And now?"

"Feels pretty good," she said. "I fell again but didn't break anything."

"Is everything okay?" I asked.

"I'm fine," she said.

"Well…I like the grey streak," I said.

"I didn't do it," she said. "It's totally natural."

We walked to a wooden bench next to a stand of pampas grass and sat down.

"It's hard to come back here," she said.

"It's hard for me too," I said. "You know me and places."

"There's too much history," she said. "It's where we met."

"And the same band was playing that night," I said. "I'm a little surprised to see you here."

"I thought you might be here," she said.

"Is that why you've avoided me?"

"It would have been too painful," she said.

"I know," I said. "There are too many places where we spent time I still can't go."

"It's been easier to stay home," she said.

"You could have changed that at any moment," I said. "I kept thinking you might show up on my doorstep."

"Not going out was easier," she said.

"And tonight?" I asked.

"I needed to see you again," she said, "and I thought you might be here."

I looked over at her, silhouetted against the dim porch light, and felt my stomach tighten into a knot. For a year I wanted to see her and get answers to what happened to us. Now that we were sitting alone together, there was none of the ease we had once enjoyed.

"You're still smoking," she said.

"Some things haven't changed," I said.

"What the hell…can I have one?" I lit her cigarette and the way the lighter lit her face reminded me what first attracted me to her. She still had a classic, almost timeless beauty that defied her age. Her eyes again drew me to her as they had done so many times before. She still looked twenty years younger than her sixty-five years. The magnetism that first drew me to her was still there. I remembered all the special moments we had shared: The kisses, the easy laughter, the softness of her skin against mine, and I wanted all of that back in my life.

For the last year I had asked myself the same unanswered questions about what had happened to us and now I was sitting alone with Rose and I was speechless. I wanted answers but, at the same time, I didn't want to break the spell of the moment with a battery of questions.

"Looks like you have a nice view of the water from your apartment," she said.

Her comment took me by surprise, because she had never been to my new apartment.

"How do you know about my view?" I asked.

"You posted pictures on your Facebook page," she said.

"That was a year ago," I said.

"I also liked the post you shared on Frank Zappa a few months ago. I really enjoyed it. He was such a good man."

I was surprised to hear she had been on my Facebook page and at the same time flattered. It was another one of her conundrums: Unfriend me then follow my postings.

Suddenly, out of the blue, she said, "I didn't like your CD."

"Nice to see you too," I said. "What didn't you like about it?"

"It was so personal."

"It was supposed to be personal. It was for you."

"That song "Midnight Snack" was just nasty."

"You didn't like hearing I wanted to taste your sweet jelly roll?"

"Exactly."

"You liked it when I was looking for your tattoo."

"But not on a CD. And you got the line wrong in 'Lost Lover's Lounge'."

"Which line?"

"The deaf mute wasn't selling trinkets," she said. "They were key chains."

"Trinkets just worked better," I said.

"The key chain was important," she said. "Like the key to your heart."

"The key to my heart?"

"Yes, that was important."

"Well, I'm sorry it was so personal and you didn't like it."

"You know me."

"I know you told perfect strangers in a club you were going to bang the beejesus out of me," I said. "But I guess that wasn't so personal."

We sat in the dark parking lot with only the drone of the music from inside the hall around us. I could feel the pressure building inside me to ask her all the questions I needed answers to, but part of me was afraid I'd scare her away if I did. And I was confused why she wanted to see me. Why after a year apart did she suddenly feel the need to talk?

"How's the Ranch?"

"Good," she said. "It's finally mine."

"And Bob's daughter?"

"I paid her off," she said.

"I'm glad you got that settled. I knew you would. It was just a matter of time."

"It's finally over."

"And the chickens?" I asked.

"They're great. Over two hundred now producing a lot of eggs."

"And your health? Are you doing okay?"

"I'm fine. Arm is still a bit stiff,"

"How's the memoir coming?"

"Good," she said.

"Is there anything I could read?"

"It's not ready yet," she said.

"I would be more than willing to help you with it…help you shape things or help with the format."

"Maybe later."

I could feel our moment slipping away, and the pressure to ask her all the questions I needed answers to building in me. It had been a year since we had talked to one another and now, out of the blue, we were sitting alone in the dark talking. It felt as though something had shifted and part of me hoped she had experienced a change of heart.

"Have dinner with me," I said.

She whirled around. "No…no…no," she said.

"I'm sure you have dinner with other friends. Why not with me?"

"No…no."

"I told you when I met you that I loved you madly," I said. "I still do. That hasn't changed."

"Can I have another cigarette?"

I lit another cigarette and handed it to her. I couldn't hold back any longer and blurted out my most pressing question.

"Why?" I said. "Why did you step away?"

We sat there in the dark and I didn't say anything; I just waited for her response. It was the one question I needed an answer to more than any other.

"Why?" I repeated. "You kept telling me we were good. Then all of a sudden you wanted me out of your life."

She cleared her throat and leaned forward. She stared off into the dark, but I could feel she wanted to tell me something, but she was struggling to let it out. I resisted saying anything more; I wanted the stillness to force her to give me the answer. She had broken my heart, and I wanted to hear the reason—the honest reason why from her. She looked over at me, leaned forward, rested her elbows on her knees, and looked off into the chilly night.

"I need to know," I said. "It all ended so abruptly with no concrete explanation."

She raised her head and looked over at me. "Because…," she said, then broke off her response and looked away.

"That's not good enough," I said.

She butted her cigarette and stared straight ahead.

"Because…you made me happy," she said softly.

I heard her words, but I couldn't speak. It was not the response I expected to hear. I replayed the word 'happy' over and over trying to understand how you could leave a loved one because they made you happy.

"You made me feel beautiful and sexy," she said, "and so very happy. I'll always love you."

"That still makes no sense," I said.

"You made me very happy," she said. "It's all I have. Don't hate me."

"I could never hate you," I said. "You're the love of my life."

"Then think of it as a proper goodbye." She stood up. "I have to go." She straightened her jacket, and we slowly started back toward her car. She had given me an answer, but it only left me more confused. Everyone wants to be happy; so why would someone purposely walk away from happiness?

"Tell me about your 'look back'," I said, as we walked.

"My what?"

"As you were leaving our street dance, you stopped and looked back at me."

"I wanted to give you a good night look," she said.

"I wish you would've stayed," I said.

"I went by Joe's Music to get another copy of your CD but they didn't have it. I want to send a copy to Joanie and Jimmy."

"Are you sure it's not too personal?"

"They'll enjoy it," she said.

"I have copies in the shop," I said. "Just stop by and I'll give you one."

“I also lost all our photos,” she said. “Somehow my computer ate them.”

“If you come by I’ll show you what I have,” I said. “Just tell me which ones you want, and I’ll send them to you.”

She opened the driver side door of her Jeep and slowly slid in. I held the door open for a moment; I wanted to postpone the end of our time together as long as possible. I wanted us to keep talking. I wanted us to return to where we once were as two people in love. It had taken so long to get to this moment I was afraid it might not happen again if I let go of the car door.

“Please have dinner with me,” I repeated.

“I can’t,” she said.

“Please.”

She gently pulled on the car door and I slowly let go. All I could do was stare in at her through the glass. She was as beautiful as the last time I saw her standing at the rear of my car the day I left the Ranch. There was so much more I wanted to know, wanted to say to her. I wanted her to know how much I missed her and how much our late night talks and moments of uncontrollable laughter meant to me. And how much I wanted to pleasure her sexually and have her surprise me with some new twist in the art of lovemaking. But I just looked in at her, wishing we had more time. She finally rolled down her window.

"I suppose you'd like me to kiss you," she said.

I smiled. "That would be nice."

She stepped out of the car, wrapped her arms around me and kissed me not once but twice. We held each other in a tight embrace for the longest time, and I was immediately reminded how good she felt in my arms. We held each other as tightly as we could for the longest time, until she finally let go of me and got back in her car. I watched her pull out of the parking lot and slowly drive away. Even though our meeting was short, we had had a conversation and the kisses. It reminded me how much I missed her and I left that night believing we would see each other again if only to give her another CD and the photos of us.

Chapter Thirty-Six

"I WANTED TO TELL YOU
BEFORE YOU HEARD ANYTHING."
- MARIAN

Rose and I had not been together for a year, but after our conversation in the Bayview Hall parking lot, it was clear we still cared for one another despite our separation. I could feel her without touching her. She had awakened something so deep in me no amount of pain could erase the indelible mark she left on me. Our brief but somewhat confusing conversation at Bayview made that clear. It also made me re-examine what I knew about love and happiness.

That night I lay in bed replaying not only what had unfolded that evening but also during our time together. The emotional and physical connection we had established was deeply imbedded in me and impossible for me to sever. Rose could choose not to continue our relationship, but she couldn't erase the impact she had on my life. She had turned my life around and shown me unconditional affection that had been absent far too long. She fed my modest talents and convinced me they had value not only to me but to someone else. She fostered my exposure to new avenues of growth: to appreciate the quiet pleasure of growing vegetables, to not being afraid to let another see my true self, to be open to speak the truths life had taught me, to believe in who I was, and to learn intimacy is not measured by its frequency, but by its depth. Revisiting all Rose had meant to me kept me awake most of the night. I was encouraged by our meeting outside the hall, hearing I had made her happy and then feeling her lips on mine. My last memory before falling asleep was Rose standing outside my 2nd Street apartment looking in on me as if to make sure I was alright.

The next day, I got to the shop and gave the place a good vacuuming and dusting in anticipation of Rose stopping by for a CD. I played a variety of conversations in my head and the questions I still wanted answered. I pulled up all the photos of Rose I had and made sure they were all in a single file. That Thursday passed without her coming by, as did Friday and the weekend.

First thing Monday morning I read a Facebook post from one of Rose's neighbors asking for prayers for a neighbor who was in the hospital. I immediately sensed who he was referring to and I quickly called Marian.

"What's going on with Rose?" I said, when she answered.

"I was just about to call you," she said. "You were next on my list."

"I just saw on Facebook she's in the hospital."

"Oh God," she said. "I wanted to tell you before you heard anything."

"Is she alright?"

"She's in intensive care and they're monitoring her."

"Is it the cancer?" I asked.

"They think she had a heart attack."

"But she's alive?" I said.

"Yes, but it is serious," Marian said. "She may have permanent kidney damage."

"Intensive Care. Okay," I said and hung up the phone.

I closed the shop and got on the next ferry off the island.

Forty-five minutes later I was in the Intensive Care unit of Providence Hospital asking the nurse in charge for Rose's room.

"Are you a relative?" she asked.

Her question stopped me cold. I looked in the room next to the nurse's station and saw Rose with tubes in her mouth, nose and her arms.

"Sir," the nurse repeated, "are you a relative?"

I slowly turned to the nurse and looked into her eyes.

"She's the love of my life," I said.

"Well…," she said, "I believe that's good enough for me."

I asked what Rose's status was and the nurse was very detailed in her explanation. Rose had suffered heart failure which had caused her kidneys to shut down, posing the threat of renal failure.

"We're just trying to ease the work of her heart," she said, "and keep her other organs working. We've sedated her so her heart doesn't have to work so hard. It doesn't look like there was any long-term kidney damage so that is good."

"Can I talk to her?"

"She can't talk," the nurse said. "We have her intubated and completely sedated. But you can certainly talk to her. We're trying to get her to come out of the sedation and see if her heart can work on its own. Hearing a familiar voice might help her come out of it."

I thanked the nurse for filling me in and I went over to the bed and gently took Rose's hand. I looked down at her with that new streak of grey in her hair and was immediately reminded just how much I missed her. I whispered her name and felt so helpless seeing how vulnerable she looked. I knelt down on the floor so I was level with her and told her repeatedly I loved her and wanted her to get well. I slowly stroked her hand and talked to her about the Ranch, the chickens and how sure I was Bella was missing her. I told her her kidneys looked good and the doctors were doing everything they could for her. She just needed to be strong and come out of the sedation.

The nurse had told me she might display some jerky behavior from the medication, and she might temporarily open her eyes. I spent the next hour talking randomly about everything that came to mind. I told her how much I enjoyed our conversation outside Bayview Hall and how sweet it was to hold and kiss her again.

The nurse came in and said they needed to run some more tests and I was welcome to come back later. I didn't feel I could do anything more while she was still sedated. I saw she was alive and resting, and I learned there was no apparent kidney damage. What Marian had originally reported as being a very serious possibility that Rose had suffered kidney damage and might possibly need to be on dialysis had turned out better than expected. I decided to leave and let Rose rest, now that I had seen her and knew more about her condition.

When I got back onto the island, I stopped by Marian's to pass on what I had learned from the nurse. We sat outside on her front porch and I gave her the better news.

"That's good to hear," Marian said."They weren't so certain earlier."

"The nurse said her kidneys and other organs looked good." I paused for a moment, reflecting on how helpless Rose looked, and I broke down and cried. The thought of possibly losing her for good was more than I could take. Even if we weren't together, I wanted her to get through this episode. There was always the chance our situation could change but only if she got better. It took me a moment to collect myself. "I hated to see her like that," I said. "She means the world to me."

"We all love her," Marian said.

"I kept telling her that. I don't know if she could hear me or not, but I had to keep telling her…in case she could."

Chapter Thirty-Seven

"He'p me...He'p me."
- Rose

Tuesdays were an optional day for me at the shop, and I decided to drive straight to the ferry that next morning to visit Rose at the hospital. When I got to the Intensive Care unit, Rose was still under sedation. The doctors had taken her breathing tubes out, which I took as a positive sign. The nurse on duty told me her heart was still a little erratic but functioning at a fairly steady rate. The nurse reconfirmed there didn't appear to be any kidney damage and her fluid outflow was good. She was confident Rose would come out of the sedation soon.

"I'm glad to hear that," I said.

"These things can take time," the nurse said. "She's basically in a fog right now. And you can see by her jerky movements she's trying to come out of it."

"Has she shown any signs of getting awake?"

"A few flickers," the nurse said. "She has opened her eyes a few times, but just for a moment. You can go in. Hearing your voice may help her along."

I went into the room and took hold of Rose's hand and rubbed it gently.

"Good morning Rose," I said softly. "It's a beautiful day outside. You should open your eyes and see it for yourself."

I continued talking to her about everything I could think of. I didn't really care what I said as long as she heard a familiar voice. I wanted her to hear me and know it was okay to come out of the sedation and rejoin us.

The nurse came up behind me with a chair. I thanked her and sat down and leaned over the bed rail so I was as close as possible to her. I continued to talk to her as I gently stroked her hair and forehead.

I saw her eyes open quickly and look at me and I repeated how much I loved her and how much I wanted her to rejoin us. She closed her eyes and twitched a bit, stretching her right leg out as if trying to get it beyond the bed rail. I ran out of things to say, so I started to sing to her. In a low voice, I sang the song I wrote for her and the Ranch called "Welcome Road." I followed up with an old blues standard "Stormy Monday" and a song I wrote for her called "Photograph Blues." She opened her eyes again and tried to sit up, but her wrist restraints kept her movements restricted.

"*He'p me,*" she said, suddenly. "*He'p me.*"

She repeated the same words she would light-heartedly say when she wanted me to help her get out of my low-riding car. But in this situation they were painful to hear.

"There's nothing I can do, babe," I said. "Just come back. It's okay."

She closed her eyes and lay back down.

I continued to talk to her over the next forty-five minutes and sang her the song I wrote about her and New Orleans:

> *"It's a rainy night in the Quarter*
> *The sidewalks glitter bright*
> *Couples in the shadows*
> *But she's not in sight"*

I kept my voice low, but loud enough for her to hopefully hear me.

> *"I know she's out there*
> *'cause the past lives on here*
> *Every corner holds promise*
> *Her ghost is everywhere."*

Again she opened her eyes briefly a few more times and twice repeated her request: "*He'p me… He'p me.*" I felt helpless. I didn't know what else to do to help her come out of her foggy state. I told the nurse what she had said and asked if she was in any pain.

"She's confused," she said, "and I'm sure it's scary. She's struggling to come out of the fog she's in. It can take some time. But it's good she was speaking."

"Do you think she knows I'm here?"

"I'm sure she does. She's just in a faraway place right now. And it can feel scary."

I was also in a faraway place. Even though we hadn't been together for a while, she was still important to me. The thought of her being incapacitated or worse reminded me of the last time I saw my mother in the hospital. She had tubes in her mouth and I could see her lips trying to form words but not producing anything I could understand. I wanted desperately to hear what she was trying to tell me, but her words never came. Her inability to tell me what she wanted to say had stayed with me ever since. I didn't want to experience that feeling again with Rose.

I stayed with Rose for another half hour with no major change in her condition. A technician came in and I was told they needed to run some more tests and I needed to leave. I decided to go back to the island and try to work.

That afternoon, Marian called and told me the doctors wanted to keep visitors to a minimum for now, and she would keep me updated on any changes.

I didn't like being shut out of seeing Rose, but I knew I wasn't 'family' despite my relationship with her. Marian had power of attorney regarding Rose's affairs, and she kept Rose's daughter, who was in Florida at the time, up-to-date on Rose's condition.

"Promise me," I told Marian over the phone, "if anything happens, you will call me."

"I will," she said.

"I would not be able to live with myself if I wasn't there for her. Promise me."

"Of course I will," she said. "I promise."

Wednesday was typically a slow day in the shop, so when I arrived, I used the time to address book business. I spent the whole day updating photos, book descriptions and responding to emails. I made a shopping list of things I needed to pick up at the grocery store before I went home for the night. At 6:30, I shut down the computer and started to leave when the phone rang.

"It's Marian…if you can," she said, "you should come to the hospital."

"What's happened?"

"You should just come now," she said, and I hung up.

Rose was not in her room when I got to the Intensive Care ward, and I asked the nurse where she was. I was told she was in surgery. I immediately texted Marian asking where she was in the building.

I found Marian and Rose's neighbor Rozie sitting at a table in the surgical waiting room on the fourth floor. There was no one else in the room except for the two of them.

"There you are," Marian said.

"Thanks for calling," I said, hugging her and then Rozie. "What's happened?"

"Her heart beat was irregular and they couldn't get it stabilized. So they took her to surgery."

"How long ago?"

"About thirty minutes."

"How serious?"

"They're working on her right now," Rozie said. "That's all we know."

The three of us sat down at a large round table and just stared at each other in disbelief. I could feel the severity of the call, and I didn't like what we were all thinking. A clergyman approached our table, asked if he could join us, and inquired if we were religious.

We told him we weren't in the strict sense of the word but his company was welcome.

"This can't be happening," I said.

"I know," Rozie said.

"We just had dinner last Saturday night," Marian said. "Rose said she felt nauseous, but we thought it was just the food."

"Did the doctor say what they were going to do?"

"Just trying to stabilize her heart" Marian said. "I've been on the phone with her daughter, so she knows what's going on."

"And she can't be here?" I said.

"She's still in Florida," Marian said. "She won't be back for a couple of days."

"So we're it?" I asked. "We're the family?"

"We're the tribe," Marian said.

"I can't believe this is happening," I said. "She opened her eyes yesterday and asked me to help her. And now this. I thought she was making progress."

"It just happened," Rozie said.

Over the intercom came the order: "Code blue… code blue…4th floor surgery."

The three of us looked at each other.

"Code blue…code blue…4th floor surgery."

"That's not good," I said.

"No it's not," Rozie said.

The three of us sat quietly at the table. All I could do was pray the doctors would get whatever Rose's issue was under control and get her back upstairs. I tried not to think about anything negative; I just wanted her to pull through this episode like she had so many times before. Even though we weren't together, I wanted her back on the island. I wanted to know she was still full of her magic and I would see her again.

"If that were the case," I heard Marian say to Rozie, "it would be for the best."

"She wouldn't want to be like that," Rozie added.

"She's a strong woman," I said. "She's beat the odds before."

"Yes, she has," Marian said.

Just then the doors to the surgical suite opened, and the surgeon came out. The three of us stood up, and his face showed no emotion, just flat and expressionless.

"I'm sorry," he said.

Marian screamed, cupped her hands over her mouth, then embraced Rozie, and they both cried uncontrollably. I just looked at the doctor. He pursed his lips and slowly shook his head. My ears plugged up, and the waiting room went quiet around me. I could see Marian and Rozie embraced and crying, but the room had no sound and no color. Everything stopped: my thoughts, the doctor's lips, the sound of friendly voices. Nothing moved or made a sound.

"I did everything I could," I finally heard the doctor say. "I tried to put in stints but they just wouldn't take. I'm so sorry."

I just stared at him in disbelief. I could hear Marian crying, but I couldn't move. I didn't want to move. I didn't want to hear what I heard or know what I knew. I wanted it to be yesterday when life was still good. I wanted the doctor's words to be a lie and for Rose to walk into the waiting room and join us. Most of all, I wanted it not to be the end.

"I truly tried everything, but her heart just gave out. I'm so very sorry."

Marian collected herself and stepped away with her phone. Rozie embraced me, and we held each other. I could hear Marian on the phone to Bethany and crying as she gave her the news. I looked over at the empty table and thought of my last words to Rose, that I loved her, and hoped she had heard them.

I waited for the news to hit me, to overtake me, and drop me to the floor, but I just felt like time had stopped. There were sounds around me, but I felt alone in the waiting room. I saw Marian finish her phone call, approach Rozie and me, then the three of us embraced.

So this is how her life ends? I thought to myself. *Alone in a cold operating room, with no friends at her side, only technicians.*

"Would anyone like to see her?" the doctor asked.

We looked at each other and Marian and Rozie both declined. I thought for a minute and, as much as I would have liked to see her one more time, I knew it wouldn't have been her. All she truly was, left her when her heart gave out.

"No," I said. "I'm fine."

"I'm going upstairs," Marian said, "and collect her things. We should have a drink for Rose."

"Sure," Rozie said. "We can go to my house."

"Are you up for a drink?" Marian asked me.

"Of course," I said.

We agreed to meet at Rozie's house on Welcome Road and have a drink to celebrate Rose.

The twenty-minute ferry ride back to the island was hard to take and felt extremely long. It also felt wrong. I felt like we were leaving Rose behind, alone in a cold place with no loved one to sit with her. I felt bad for leaving her, that I should have stayed with her until her daughter returned to take control of her body. It felt wrong to just drive away and leave the woman I loved so deeply to lay there alone, like I no longer cared about her. I knew we all cared about her, but it just felt wrong to leave her alone. Rose deserved better. She deserved to live and continue to bring joy into other lives, not to be left alone in a cold place with no loved ones with her as she journeyed on.

I had been with my father when he died and, as sad as his passing was, it wasn't as devastating to me as Rose's death. My father and I had managed, in his last years, to mend a lot of old wounds and enjoy each other's company. But I still felt Rose and I had unfinished business, and now she was gone and with her all my unanswered questions.

It wasn't until the following day that her death hit me. I just sat in my shop with the door locked and the lights off and cried like a baby. All that we had together was decidedly over. There was no chance to talk again. She would not finish her memoir, and she would not see the photos of us she had lost. There would be no more kisses in the dark, no Saturday steak night, no more opportunities to find that tattoo. There was no more anything with Rose, and I felt like all the life in me had vanished with her death.

Chapter Thirty-Eight

"Her ghost is everywhere."
- "The Rose of Bourbon Street"

No one likes to think about death, especially the death of a loved one. We avoid it for good reason: Death marks the physical end of all we were, whatever we were destined to do in this life, the lives we were meant to impact, the love we had to give and receive. Death is the end of the plans we have for ourselves and the end of our physical life with others. Rose's death left a huge hole in my life and forced me to examine what our year together meant. She had given me back my sense of worth and helped me to re-emerge from the dark hole I had allowed myself to exist in. I owed Rose my life, and I felt cheated out of the joy I believed we could have still brought each other. But that was not meant to be, and I was left to continue on without her in my life. And that was something I didn't want to think about.

Rose's memorial was scheduled for late October 2016 at the Comfort Winery, just down the street from the Ranch. It had been a year since I had driven down Wilkinson Road, and it was hard to pass Rose's little market and feel the absence of her in my life and all the glorious months I had spent on the Ranch. The winery sits on a beautiful bluff overlooking Saratoga Passage, and all of Rose's island friends and family were invited.

I had been asked by Marian to send any photos of Rose I had so she could forward them to Rose's daughter for a PowerPoint presentation of Rose's life. I sent a dozen nice pictures I had of Rose and the two us together. I was also asked about Rose's musical preferences to accompany the slides. I said she loved Frank Zappa, Cajun music in general, and she really liked Little Feat.

When I arrived at the winery, I was immediately greeted by a woman in her forties. I recognized something familiar in her welcoming eyes and full lips.

"You must be David," she said. "I recognized the hat. I'm Bethany."

It took me a minute to connect with the name and, at the same time, take in the beautiful facial features I had known in Rose.

"It's wonderful to finally meet you," I said. "I see your mother in your eyes and smile."

We embraced, and I found it hard to let go of her.

"I'm so sorry," I said. "Your mother was very special to me."

"Thank you," she said.

"I had hoped to meet you earlier, under better circumstances, but your mother…well…we never got to that place."

"I understand," she said. "But it's nice to meet you now."

"It's so uncanny," I said. "I see your mom in you. And it makes me feel… good inside."

"Marian said you're going to sing today?"

"It seemed appropriate," I said.

The members of Rose's island tribe arrived and it was good to see all her friends who had become mine after we got together. The PowerPoint presentation of Rose's life, with Little Feat playing in the background, painted a wonderful picture of Rose throughout the years. I was struck by how beautiful she was as a young woman, and how much of her youthful allure stayed with her into her sixties. She could have easily been a model throughout her life. She had kept her svelte figure, and her youthful facial features had not been lost over the decades. I couldn't help feel how lucky I was to have loved and been loved by such a beautiful woman. But it was the non-photographic aspects of her life that were not transmitted in the presentation that struck me the deepest. We didn't hear her voice and her easy laugh or her wry sense of humor. Missing was her playfulness, the tender moments we shared, or the way she would unleash the sensual dancer in her when she heard a song that tapped her inner rhythms. There was none of the playful banter that unfolded while cleaning eggs or making dinner for two. None of these aspects of Rose were captured in the photos; they were merely static moments without the soul of the subject.

I kept waiting for the pictures of us that showed her happy and playful to pop up but there was only picture after picture of every other phase of her life. Finally towards the end, one picture taken of us in the dark Blue Nile Club in New Orleans appeared; we were the epitome of two Bohemians wearing sunglasses and looking flatly into the camera.

When the slide show ended, several close friends got up and shared anecdotes of Rose, followed by

Marian who spoke eloquently about her long friendship with Rose.

I was the last to speak, but I didn't have any anecdotes to share; no single remembrance that would reflect who Rose was to me or the depth of her personality. All I had was a mystery to offer. I had spent several days trying to make sense of our time together and what she had meant to me, but I couldn't find the words to express all I felt and everything I had lost when she died. There were just too many poignant moments, revealing conversations and intimacies shared to condense into a meaningful anecdote. And to be honest, at that moment, I wasn't sure what our year together added up to.

Something very special had transpired with us; I felt that deep down inside me, but it was hard to articulate what it was. I was still too confused over her sudden death to make sense of our time together. Because we had more than a romance; we shared an experience that went much deeper than kisses, love making and laughter. In the time we knew each other, I was with her almost every day, and I was allowed into her life like few others, especially in terms of intimacy.

So when it came time to sum up my thoughts and feelings for Rose, the overriding word that kept coming to mind was: Fate.

This is for Bethany, I began my eulogy.
I loved your mother more than anyone else in my life. But in every life and love there are mysteries, illusive clues and answers left unsaid. Having said that, I do not believe in coincidences. I believe things happen for a reason. There was a reason Rose and I met two years ago September 2014 at the final Bayview Street dance. There was a reason I went to the Ranch two days later and we spent two hours talking. There was a reason she let me into her life and her heart even while still dealing with the unexpected loss of her husband Bob. There was a reason she invited me to go to New Orleans with her after knowing me for only a month. There is a reason we loved each other as passionately as we did for a year. And that reason lies in the heart.

There is also a reason why she pulled away from me…it was out of fear, a close friend speculated. There is a reason why she stayed away so long from the place where we first met. It was too painful, she told me, and I felt that same pain.

There is a reason she made an exception and came to our Bayview gig two months ago. There is a reason that two weeks later…on the two year anniversary of our first meeting she returned to the place where we first met. There is a reason we were both there at the same time. And there is a reason she took me aside that night and finally spoke from her heart. I asked her why...why the separation and she said: "Because you made me happy." She thanked me for making her feel beautiful and sexy. There is a reason I told her how much I loved her. There is a reason I couldn't take my eyes off her when she got into her car that night. She was that beautiful, and I wasn't sure when we would have another moment like that. There is a reason she rolled down her window and said: "I suppose you'd like me to kiss you?"

There is a reason she got out of the car and hugged and kissed me that night...not once but twice...for the last time. There is a reason that one week after our last meeting she passed away. And there is a reason that my last words to her in the hospital were "I love you Rose." And there is a reason I will love Rose until my last breath. In each case, the reason lies in the heart. New Orleans was an important place for both of us—the place that solidified our relationship. So it is only fitting that my musical tribute to Rose be in a song I wrote for her set in our New Orleans.

When I finished my eulogy, I sang "The Rose of Bourbon Street" which summed up how I felt about Rose and where we both were now.

It's a rainy night in the Quarter
sidewalks glitter bright
couples in the shadows
but she's not in sight

I know she's out there
the past lives on here
every corner holds promise
Her ghost is always near

So I'm looking for that woman
who cannot be found
we were once lovers
High on this town
So I keep looking...for the Rose...
of Bourbon Street

Signs of love's decay
in all she had to say
it's a cold proposition
played out every day

I'm looking for that woman
who cannot be found
we were once lovers
High on this town
So I keep looking...for the Rose...
of Bourbon Street

Promises numb the heart
like a cold wind off Canal St
lazy rhythms on Frenchman
No time to sleep

I'm looking for that woman
who cannot be found
we were once lovers
High on this town
So I keep looking...for the Rose...
of Bourbon Street

With the conclusion of the song, the memorial came to a close. Bethany came up to me from the rear of the hall and hugged me.

"That was really beautiful," she said. "I didn't know."

"It was your mother who was truly beautiful… inside and out."

"She never spoke of you," Bethany said.

"I'm not surprised," I said. "There were many things we didn't get to."

"I wish I had used more of your photographs, but I just didn't know. Especially the one you said she really liked…the one on Bourbon Street."

"She thought she looked her best," I said. "And she did. It was a wonderful trip, and we were very happy."

"I can tell from what you said and from the song," she said. "I just didn't know."

"You and me both," I said.

Chapter Thirty-Nine

"It's not that the dead do not speak. It's just that we have forgotten how to listen."
- Pier Paolo Pasolini

The ensuing weeks and months were a period of pain and reflection for all of Rose's friends and for me. The woman I had loved more than anything in the world was gone, and I was still alive. It somehow didn't feel fair. I had waited my whole life to find the love and joy I had with Rose only to have it end so abruptly and without apparent cause.

She had stepped away from me without any signs of discontent or unsuitability and a year later died. There were things I still needed to know and day after day the questions dominated my waking hours, and Rose was never far from my daily thoughts. Gone was the possibility of ever seeing her again, of finding her tattoo, or ever speaking with her. She had left so many things unsaid which was one of the perplexing things about her. When we were together, I found her vagaries alluring and I felt in time what she didn't say early on would eventually be revealed the longer we knew each other. I never felt the need to be confrontational when she told me, "I didn't get to it" in my previous books. I believed, in time, she would tell me exactly what she meant and we would address the subject then. But time was not our friend, and I still had questions: Why was she so adamant about separating if I made her happy? Why couldn't she continue writing her memoir with me still in her life? What was she truly afraid of?

I remember the brief conversation I had with her neighbor Rozie when Rose had her bladder cancer.

"I think she was afraid," Rozie had said.

"Afraid of what?"

"I'm not sure."

"Did she tell you she was afraid?"

"No, it was just my impression. I just think she was afraid."

Remembering that exchange with Rozie made me recall Rose standing in her doorway the night of our first date wearing her tight red dress. Red was clearly Rose's color. The feeling the color red triggered in me spanned a range of emotions whether imagined or real: passion and happiness at one end and danger and fear at the opposite extreme.

Rose could have been afraid for any number of reasons: fearful of losing another person she loved, fearful of being so involved with someone she would not write her life story, afraid to let go and completely love another man, fearful of not being remembered. Perhaps she was afraid if we continued with our life together and something happened to her I would have been tied to a diminished version of herself, and so afraid of losing her appeal, I might leave her. These were all possible reasons Rose could have been afraid, but unfortunately I never found out for sure from her.

Two months after Rose died, my spiritual guide Cherub came into my book shop to see how I was doing.

"I wanted to come by earlier," she said, "but I knew you were still healing. How are you?"

"I'm getting by," I said. "It's been a hard stretch."

"I'm very sorry," she said. "It sounded like you were very happy together."

"We were," I said. "But I still have a lot questions that have been left unanswered."

"I know," she said.

She reminded me of a death that still haunted her. The six-year old daughter of her best friend was tragically crushed by a fallen tree on Christmas Day five years earlier. The little girl was like her own child, Cherub said, and she had taken the death as hard as the little girl's parents.

"It's been five years," Cherub said, "and I still haven't gotten over it."

"I can't imagine feeling like this for five years."

"It will get better," she said, "and now you know you can love and be loved. Things happen for a reason. There is energy around us, and you will know what to do with it."

She offered a fresh blessing on the shop and gave me another big hug. As she stepped out my shop door, she turned and said: "Be mindful of feathers in your path," she said.

"Excuse me."

"White feathers especially," she said. "They are your guardian angel…a loved one, speaking to you. And dimes. Watch for dimes in your path."

"Why dimes?" I asked.

The number ten is powerful," Cherub said.

"Ten," I said. "That's how many months we were actually together."

"Ten represents completion… totality…unity"

The following day, I took a break from uploading books and went out to the parking lot behind my shop. I walked to my car, leaned against the rear hatch, and took a deep breath. The November air was crisp with a hint of moisture from the on-shore breeze that signaled a change in the weather. I casually looked down and there at my feet was a small white feather. I stared at it for a moment then slowly bent down and picked up the feather. I rolled the quill between my thumb and forefinger and thought about what Cherub had told me to be aware of the previous day. I had not encountered any feathers before that day and had no recollection of seeing any on the ground, especially at my feet outside my car. I didn't have an immediate answer why the feather would suddenly appear to me, but I did know how I felt about coincidences. I couldn't bring myself to discard it. I took off my hat and stuck the feather in the cloth band.

Over the next two weeks, I encountered another nine white feathers in my path. The tenth one appeared on a blustery morning when once again I was standing at the rear of my car. With the strong wind blowing in off Saratoga Passage, leaves and bits of paper skittered across the parking lot. Out of the corner of my eye I saw a small white object drifting over the blacktop. I followed its wispy dance toward me then it suddenly stopped at my feet. The wind gusted, threatening to take off my hat. Leaves and part of a napkin rustled by, but the feather did not move. I picked it up and admired its tenacity against the swirling wind and carefully added it to my hat band. I couldn't help thinking the feathers, all ten of them, were more than just an accident. And for just a moment I remembered Rose leaning against the rear of my car, moisture streaks on her face, when I left the Ranch for the last time.

Rose's daughter, Bethany, and I had been in contact via email for several days after the memorial. For good reason, she was still very upset at her mother's passing but for different reasons than Rose's island friends and me. I had shared with her my experience with Rose, but unfortunately Bethany knew a different woman than I did. As a young mother, Rose had given Bethany up; for whatever reasons Rose could not embrace motherhood, and I could hear the pain and anger in Bethany's emails.

I learned from those who had known Rose longer than me that she was not without her own checkered past. I was told Rose was still married to the man named Ben when she moved in with her late husband Bob, and that Ben had later died of a heart attack.

When Bethany was young, Rose took her from the only parents she had known and moved to Alaska. Eventually Rose returned Bethany to her step-parents, but the trail of abandonment had one more chapter in Rose's life; and I was, to some degree, the last in that procession.

Love is a mysterious emotion. It can make you do extraordinary things, make sacrifices that do not come easy. When we encounter love, we don't always know what to do with it; when we feel love, we fear losing it. When we accept love, no one can take it away no matter how hard they try. Love is the reason we live, and its absence can be our death. It's love's mysterious nature that keeps us alive.

As angry and hurt as I had been with Rose stepping away from me and what I felt was our good life together, I felt it was less personal than it was the way she dealt with the fear of getting too close to something or someone she could lose. I sensed no weakness in her when she stepped away from me. Her quivering voice did defy her words, but her eyes were devoid of any vicious intent or bitterness. Only the moisture streaks in the dust on her cheeks defied her decision. I quickly realized Bethany and I knew a different Rose, and my emails were not easing her pain. We suspended our exchanges until the tenth feather crossed my path.

When I got back in the shop after encountering that tenth white feather, I sent Bethany an email about what Cherub had told me about the feathers and the dimes. I told her how many feathers had suddenly appeared in my path, and she immediately wrote back.

"Oh my God," she wrote. "I've been finding dimes ever since the memorial."

I knew Bethany had had a different experience with her mother than me, but that didn't alter how I felt about either of them. I understood Bethany's anger that she had been given up as a baby and Rose had never been a mother in her life. But I had experienced a different side of Rose.

I came to realize every relationship Rose had with those closest to her was different, and they appeared to be compartmentalized. The stories she told her various friends were often similar, but not always the same factually. There were clearly events in her past that were too painful to confront, especially those concerning her daughter. Guilt can be a powerful deterrent to closeness, especially when you are unable to express remorse or regret. Perhaps Rose sought to right the wrongs, of her early life, by trying to be a better person to those people she met later in life. Maybe that was her way of making amends; accepting who she once was, knowing she couldn't change her youthful actions, but also striving to be that better person, much like the old bluesman she identified with in New Orleans.

Rose had shown me love and affection and a willingness to expand my life experience through her own. She had opened herself up to me in so many ways which allowed me to be as open and revealing as I have ever been with anyone. I was willing to literally stand naked before her when I had no rational reason to do so. She brought out the trust in me that was not my natural response to a relative stranger. She saw a higher purpose in me than I had ever seen in myself and for that I would be eternally grateful. Every life is a mystery, but not every mystery calls us to solve it. That was not the case when it came to understanding my time with Rose.

I've led a life of frequent sorrow; some of my own doing, some of it from others. I have known moments of joy, but the deepest satisfaction had eluded me. I have known disappointment in myself and in the actions of others. But through the worst of times, I have sought pleasure and joy, and the best in others. I have been a pleasure seeker and a life traveler. Sorrow has known my name, but not always my path. Pain knows where I have been, but not always where I'm going. My path has been a life of seeking, not for treasure or wealth, but for the simplest of fortunes found only in the heart of another.

The only thing I have ever wanted from life was one more breath and a chance to experience another day of happiness doing what brings me pleasure. With Rose, I found that fortune if for only the briefest time. True love does exist, I learned, and not just in the young. Sometimes you have to live a lifetime to truly appreciate or embrace an honest love, a love that is a gift.

It took encountering those ten white feathers in my path for me to find some of the answers I had been seeking for over a year. Rose had been my teacher, my best friend, my lover and my muse, and I believe I had provided her what she needed most and what had been missing in her life. She had shown me unconditional love and affection, and I had reciprocated. She told me I made her feel beautiful and sexy, and she gave me permission to be my true self. But, in the end, she was willing to step away from someone who made her happy to fulfill her journey…to not be forgotten.

After Rose's memorial, I asked Marian if she had seen the memoir Rose was working on among her things around the house. She told me there were random sheets of paper and scraps of notes in her things but nothing in the way of a formal manuscript. I had secretly hoped Rose had left us an accounting of her life, a life she so adamantly wanted to document and perhaps be remembered for. But such was not the case. All the remembering and recounting she had been working on for well over a year had not materialized into a formal document. And a part of me was sad there was nothing concrete to show for the life she had lived or an accounting of her vivacious spirit that touched anyone she befriended.

It became clear to me in April of 2017 that my calling was to ensure her wish to be remembered. It was up to me to write her story as I knew it. Obviously, I could not write the story she planned to write; only she could have done that. But I could write her story as I knew her—what I saw, what she shared with me, and the effect her life had on at least one other human being. Hopefully, my recounting of the time we spent together would serve as a microcosm of a larger life lived: Shed a light on a life not easily revealed. I felt I owed Rose that much for giving me back my life.

I do not believe in coincidences: Not the good, the bad, or the unexplainable when it comes to love and life. They both happen for a reason. We only need to be open to receive them both. I am certain I knew Rose long before I ever met her; that I had felt her before I first touched her. It was as though we had both lived our separate lives and were waiting for each other, waiting for that moment when our lives would intersect again and complete the journeys we were both on. I believe I was someone she needed in the final chapter of her life. She needed to be deeply and honestly loved, and she needed to know her life had made a difference. Neither of us needed to be changed; we just needed to be appreciated and loved and allowed to grow. And on that account, she had made a difference. She renewed my belief in love and shared with me all the affection she had to give. I couldn't have asked for anything more.

I never did find Rose's tattoo, but it was not for a lack of searching. I told her so just before I left the Ranch, and her response was just as enigmatic.

"Are you sure," she said.

"Pretty sure," I said. "I've seen every inch of you and still no tattoo."

"Clearly you weren't looking in the right place."

"Trust me," I said, "I looked from head to toe and found nothing."

"It's there," she said. "But you have to find it for yourself."

"Are you trying to seduce me one last time?" I said.

She smiled. "As much as I would love to," she said, "sex would complicate things."

"And we don't need any more complications?"

"Trust me," she said, "you'll find it and you'll know what it means. It will be as permanent as ink."

Post Script

"If you go back far enough,
you eventually get to the root of it."

I don't believe it is a coincidence the character Motherbright in my first memoir — *In Different Times* — came into my life briefly when I was eighteen. She too was a seeker and teacher. She was a beautiful, alluring, mature woman and something of a mysterious figure during, what was for me, a time of turmoil and confusion. Why she briefly came into my life at that time may have been a coincidence or it may have been for a specific reason. Perhaps to plant a seed that would take a lifetime to mature. Then in my sixth decade, Motherbright's mirror in the person of Rose appeared when I most needed a guiding light.

Like the meaning of finding a dime in your path, a good life reflects completion, coming full circle, with a sense of unity. And in between, if we have lived fully, we love, we learn, we teach, and we allow others to flourish through us. Rose accomplished all of those things with me and others in her life, and I believe I provided her what she needed most from me. I'm certain everyone who knew Rose walked away from knowing her with a meaningful lesson to take with them in their life. It is up to each of us to discover that lesson for ourselves. Rose lived in the moment, the here and now; perhaps because a part of her past was too painful to live with. To make up for her inability to erase the past, she created a new life and filled every present moment with as much passion and joy as possible.

My brief life with Rose was at times cryptic; answers were often hinted at, not always explained. The answers were left up to me to discover, because they would be the *only* honest answers. If you were lucky enough to be in her tribe, you were subject to a learning experience whether you immediately recognized it or not. Our meeting was no coincidence; we were twin flames that burned bright. We were perfect mirrors of one another, reflecting what was good in the other as well as dispelling any fears that would prevent us from fulfilling our appointed journeys.

In my play *The Old Guitar Player*, which received a production grant from the same Seattle arts organization Rose once worked for, there is a character named Malo the Fool. Malo is both the narrator and the voice of the human spirit. He is dressed in black and as he says in the opening scene: *"There is nothing neutral about this color. It may seem mournful but does not the light emerge from darkness? Black is the germinal stage of all life. Think of Man…the predominance of carbon in him. Is it not carbon, crystallized by pressure, which produces the diamond?"*

I will always see Rose as a diamond crystallized by life and the dark moments that informed her life. In the end, the time Rose and I had together was more than a series of isolated moments. It has taken me time and much introspection to realize there was a deeper meaning to our relationship. I was her witness, and she was mine. We both had expressed needs and our brief time together was essential to finding what had been missing in our lives. It was our time to share, to grow, to learn, to teach, to make each other laugh with ease, and mend the fractures that had defined our lives for so long. It was our season to love and be loved, so we could be reminded how wonderful being loved felt one more time.

I believe, when Rose stepped away from me, she knew something was happening inside her; the tumor that had been growing in her clearly signaled changes in her body. The repeated falls she experienced furthered that message, followed ultimately by a heart that failed her. What she chose to do with what was happening inside her explains many things: her focus on writing down moments in her life on scraps of paper before they were lost, having one last dinner with Marian, and seeking me out to tell me I had made her happy. Everything that occurred happened for a reason, and it was up to me to understand that reason and accept the lessons our brief life together provided.

In the end, I believe what remains of each of us is our story—not just the events, but the impact we had on others, the difference we made in another life. And those stories have to be told or else they are forgotten. As we unfold the life of another, we also expose the indelible truths in ourselves: we learn, we discover, and we grow. Once written down, that life will not soon be forgotten. So I share this story of Rose Rydeen and our time together so that love's mystery may endure for more than just a season.

The Beginning

Made in the USA
Columbia, SC
26 July 2019